JOURNEY TO A GOVERNED WORLD

Thru 50 Years in The Peace Movement

by
Lucile W. Green

Acknowledgements

I want to express my special gratitude to Benjamin Ferencz for taking time from his busy schedule to advise me in the early stages of preparing manuscript for this book. And many thanks to Keith Beggs for editing and proofreading and for his valuable suggestions along the way. To Ross Smyth of Montreal, Canada I am indebted for corrections and additions that expanded the scope of the book. To my former student, Blythe Anderson Lucero and folks at Blythe Spirit in Richmond, CA my appreciation for the long and tedious computer work, and to Lee Graphics in Albany, CA for the cover design.

Finally, I am grateful for the optimism of The Uniquest Foundation that made this early edition of the book possible.

Second printing 1992
Copyright © 1991 by Lucile W. Green
All rights reserved
Printed in the United States of America
Library of Congress Catalog Card Number
91-68112
ISBN 0-9631720-1-8

THE UNIQUEST FOUNDATION
One Lawson Road
Berkeley, California
94707 USA

TABLE OF CONTENTS

LIST OF ILLUSTRATIONS:
Cartoons and Logos

FOREWORD

It is an ancient Chinese adage that a journey of a thousand miles begins with just one step. That presumes, of course, that one is heading in the right direction. Lucile Green spent her most formative years in China. From the writings of such learned philosophers as Laotzu and Confucius and her experiences as a missionary's daughter in a foreign land she developed a rare perception that human beings everywhere, regardless of cultural differences, share a common desire to live in harmony with nature and their neighbors. As a teacher of philosophy and the humanities she shared her wisdom with her students and developed her own perceptions of the steps and direction required to reach her vision of a peaceful international society.

Here she recounts her fifty-year journey to a governed world. It is a chronicle of one dedicated individual striving against impossible odds to make a difference by changing the way people think about world problems. But it is more than that. She speaks to the reader through a long series of articles and lectures delivered over the past thirty years. Each one remains fresh and timely—and an important guide to the traveler still searching for a more rational way to manage this planet.

She describes her early involvement, the very different approaches by scholars and laymen seeking the right road to peace, the attempts to outlaw and abolish war, and the movement toward a governed world. Certain fundamental themes reappear in the writings she now shares: disarmament, the important role of women, world law, the United Nations, a more democratic approach to world organization, a historical view of the disarmament process, the growing interdependence of nations, the need for world federation and measures essential to preserve the environment.

World leaders and all those seeking a "new world order" can gain a great deal from the insights shared in this perceptive book. In her concluding section, Lucile Green recognizes that this is "only one earth and it's in our hands." Her personal assessment is tainted by anguish as she recalls our past history of slavery, feuding colonies, warfare, human degradation and Hiroshima. Yet she remains filled with hope that as individuals and groups everywhere stand up for their human rights a democratic federal world government can soon be reached. She calls upon and inspires the reader to take an active role in shaping one civilized world community with liberty, justice and a healthy environment for all.

The journey of Lucile Green, recounted through her essays, points the reader in the right direction and says, through its example and exhortation, "Never despair, each one of you can take us one step closer to a more humane world for everyone."

Benjamin B. Ferencz
Former Nuremberg War Crimes Prosecutor
Author of books on International Law
Co-author of Planethood

PREFACE

Having lived my early years as a "foreigner" in China, my first impression on arriving, at the age of ten, in America was "Why, they're ALL foreigners here!"

To my eyes China had been a vast landscape with human touches–clustered villages and walled towns, temples with curving roofs, and here and there an arched bridge, a roadside shrine, or a round moon-gate accentuating the landscape, sometimes in loving caricature of nature. Poor but happy people blended into or emerged from that landscape.

By contrast, America seemed a scene of bustling activity–of rampant civilization with nature confined to reservations called "parks," or reduced to lining city lawns and boulevards. People everywhere, going everywhere.

I know now that these were both impressions of an outsider who, as a child of two cultures, had never really belonged to either. As I grew older, these impressions were somewhat shaped by understanding, but never fundamentally changed. My last two years in China were spent as a student at Yenching University (now Beijing University) where I studied, among other things, the ancient Chinese philosophers, Laotzu and Confucius. They reinforced my image of an ideal "Yin-Yang" balance between the natural environment and human civilization. At the same time I witnessed the early rumblings of change in the student demonstrations of 1933-35 against the Japanese invasion of Northern China.

At the age of eighteen I returned, finally, to America to finish my education. I made the transition here from "MD" (Missionaries' Daughter) to BA, MA and PhD, assimilating the great western tradition of humanistic philosophy (not much of nature there either!) When, in 1935-37, some college students were sought by the Quakers for an "Emergency Peace Campaign," I volunteered and spent two summers in rural America learning from my peers about people, ideas and issues, and about the cause that became a central focus in my life. As I look back, I think it may be because I grew up somewhat adrift from moorings in both Eastern and Western cultures that I attached myself so early to the peace movement. The same may be true of my attraction to the idea of world citizenship, an identity and commitment beyond traditional boundaries of nation, race and creed. These two ideas, deepened and sharpened by years of teaching philosophy and the humanities, have given me a sense of purpose and belonging. They have shaped the direction of a journey that has taken more than fifty years. This book is a record of that journey.

Actually, this book started by accident. After fifty years in the movement, I was sorting through hundreds of notes, articles, and speeches when I decided, for no particular reason, to arrange them in chronological order. To my astonishment I found that they reflected–not only a personal odyssey through the most critical of times in human history, but also a sort of living history of that time when the future of all life on this planet was uncertain. Here were ideas and events, some of the raw material of history, spanning the period of the Mutual Assured Destruction ("MAD") policy of the Cold War (see *Testimony on Fallout Shelters*,) to talk of "New World Order" (see *Roots of a World Democracy*).

Other people will write histories of this period, each from the point of view of the author, for histories are necessarily selective. As in the past, most of them will probably revolve around power struggles of the elite. For them this book has little to offer. But things are changing. Now that the arsenals of power are catastrophic–ultimately suicidal, the "games" of a few in high places seem strangely hollow. But mass media have turned ordinary people by the millions into determined activists–witness the democracy movements all over the world. Moved by ideas of "freedom," "rights," "a better life," "a sustainable environment," they have confronted the arsenals of power–and won. The time may be at hand when histories will deal more with ordinary people and events, and with the contest of ideas. To them this book can make a contribution.

Meanwhile, this personal account may serve several purposes:

To those doughty veterans of the peace and environment movements, it may provide a historical context and some lessons from the past (for example, in *The New Abolitionists: Some Lessons from the 19th Century*). It may also offer insights into the process and dynamics of the movement as viewed, rightly or wrongly, from my perspective (see *Convergence: the High Road and the Low Road*).

iv

Environmentalisis may note the early formulation of a basis for ecological ethics (in *From Territorial to Ecological Imperative*).

To those later joiners who feel overwhelmed by the truly formidable obstacles ahead, it may give heart to see how far we have come in just one lifetime. "Peace," which was hardly an issue in the '30's, was "unAmerican" in the '50's and only became a "movement" in the '60's, is now a global force to be reckoned with by the nations. While I write, events in Europe and Asia seem to show the *people's* movements unstoppable. Ecology, which was an unfamiliar word until the '70's, has become a major unifying concern of people and nations–witness the attention focused on the United Nations Conference on Environment and Development in Brazil in 1992. And world government, which was anathema even to the peace movement until the '90's, has been put on the global agenda by the Stockholm Initiative for a Commission on Global Governance (note developments in *A Constitution for the World?*). Peace demonstrations, which in my experience in the '30's consisted of a dozen or so Quakers with a few Methodists and Unitarians, now number in the millions all over the world. We have come a LONG way!

Finally, and most important to me, this book if nothing else is a legacy to the children, especially my grandchildren, Julia, Claudia, Felix, Ismael and Jesse, who will inherit this beautiful, beleaguered planet.

PART I

EARLY INVOLVEMENT

TESTIMONY ON FALLOUT SHELTERS

Deeply concerned about the issues of war and peace, I eagerly responded to the call, "Women Strike for Peace". Women couldn't be accused of communist sympathy just for being women, I thought. I was mistaken, and I acquired a modest file with the FBI. I became involved with the movement and was chosen to represent the Women-for-Peace position on fallout shelters for the schools in California. This was a period when, to make the military policy of "Mutual Assured Destruction" (MAD) credible to the other side (USSR), an all-out effort was launched to persuade American citizens to build underground shelters to "survive" a thermonuclear war.

I speak as a member of the coordinating committee of WOMEN FOR PEACE of the East Bay Area, part of a spontaneous grass-roots movement for disarmament and peace which began November first, 1961, and is now spreading round the world. Our movement started because preservation of life is the primeval instinct of women, and life is now totally threatened.

We are mothers, most of us, of the children you are proposing to protect by building fallout shelters in new schools. We have a lot at stake: our children's lives, of course, and also the quality of life we want them to inherit, and something we call democracy, which includes reverence for human life everywhere, and the rule of justice under law.

We do not want the kind of protection for our children that is being proposed here. We oppose this legislation for many reasons:

- First, it is shockingly unrealistic.
- Second, it is *not* "a kind of insurance".
- Third, it will tend to give a false sense of security to the unthinking, encouraging the myth that surviving a thermonuclear war is possible.
- Fourth, it could thus make our leaders and the Russians believe it would be politically "safe" to engage in war, and

---

*To the joint committee on New School Building Shelter Facilities of the State of California. January 29, 1962.

1

thus actually increase the likelihood of war.

• Fifth, it is an alternative, psychologically and economically, to an all-out program to achieve a disarmed world by multilateral negotiated disarmament–a goal we firmly believe is possible were we to put the research, money, energy and will into this effort that we are now putting into war preparations, including civil defense.

First then, it is unrealistic. It will protect neither our children, nor the environment, nor our way of life. We women have done our homework. We have read the pamphlet *Fallout Protection* and other Civil Defense material. We have also read *Consumer's Report, Scientific American, Bulletin of the Atomic Scientists, Saturday Review,* and books by scientists on radiation and the effects of thermonuclear war. We have read the *Congressional Hearings* at which the misgivings of scientists for the kind of program which is proposed here have been expressed. We know the assumptions on which shelter construction is based are unrealistic. One five-megaton bomb exploded at or near ground level is used as the basis for describing the effects of thermonuclear war! How misleading this is for a region like the Bay Area in which there are no less than 27 military targets! We know that cities are commonly admitted to be doomed in an all-out nuclear war. We do not wish to spend millions of dollars constructing our children's tombs.

And why assume an attack will be by *nuclear* bombs? It could as well be by chemical or biological weapons. In this case, according to former chief chemical officer of the U.S. Army, General Creasy, shelters would guarantee sure death, "since the ventilating systems will conveniently arrange that all citizens in underground shelters be quickly exterminated." (*The New Republic,* 10-23-61)

And what about weapons of the future? How deep would you dig to protect our children from the Asteroid Bomb of the 1970's — that "continent-shattering weapon" with an explosion "1,000 times as great as the energy of a multi-megaton bomb." (*Berkeley Gazette,* 1-18-62)

Second, it is not a "kind of insurance." There is no actuarial basis for calling this shelter program an "insurance." The latter

2

implies that there is some kind of pay-off by a surviving society for a calamity striking part of that society. Who will pay off in a thermo-nuclear war? And who will there be to collect if the shelters don't work? Can anyone insure health as the pitiful remnants emerge from the shelters to radioactive ruins? Can anyone insure the balance of Nature's forces after such a holocaust — with withered plants, dead birds and animals and fish?

Let me refer you to the historic report of the American Association for the Advancement of Science issued this December, (*Science*, 12-29-61) which I have appended for your convenience, and from which I quote briefly:

"In general, the development of a shelter program cannot greatly influence the conclusion, namely, that a massive nuclear attack would have the immediate effect of destroying the social structure. A particular shelter system is designed to resist a certain assumed intensity of attack, and its success depends on the validity of this assumption. But an opponent can be expected to respond to such a defensive move by stepping up the intensity of attack. Any shelter system short of one that places the nation's entire population and industry permanently underground can be negated by a corresponding increase in the attacker's power...

'If we consider in its entirety the problem of recovery from nuclear war, there is, we believe no scientific basis at present for a useful prediction of what kind of society — if any — would emerge from the ruins. If society embarks on the path of nuclear war, science cannot now offer enlightenment on the end result.

'We must conclude that society can no longer be defended by an unlimited war. If we permit such a war to occur in the future course of human history, we run the risk of ending human history altogether. Peace, which was until now a human *want*, has become a human *need*."

Third, this legislation therefore gives a false sense of security that communities "would be able to return to tolerable living conditions" above ground in a comparatively short time. The pretty picture (*Fallout Protection* p. 38) of neatly uniformed men hosing down a tidy city street with "clean" water, a shiny fire engine in the background and the American flag flying, insults the intelligence of informed people! Even if we could survive an attack, assuming for the moment it is a nuclear one, and the ensuing firestorms which would consume the oxygen for thousands of square miles and lay waste the land, — *if* we could survive the blast, the heat, the suffocation of the first two weeks and come out of the shelter, and *if* at that time the radiation had attenuated to the "tolerable" level of one roentgen per hour (based on the most optimistic, and we feel unrealistic estimate of conditions) this one roentgen per hour should be compared to the Maximum Permissible Limit, which is .16 roentgens per year! This figure, set by the Federal Radiation Council in 1960, is for protection of the general public against radiation causing physical damage only. The level for protection against genetic damage is one-third of this. (See safety code issued by President Eisenhower May 16, 1960.) This means that on coming out of the shelter the survivors would receive in ten minutes the Maximum Permissible Limit of radiation for a whole year! How "tolerable" a living condition is this? Because we doubt the assumptions behind this proposal, we have no faith in its plan to protect us or our children. But even more–and this is **our fourth objection –we fear every move in the direction of making war more "acceptable" to the general public is making war more probable.**

A large-scale government-sponsored program of building shelters under the public schools would, by giving the illusion of minimizing the risks and increasing the chances for survival, make this country "safe"–from what? From Communist attack? If we were in their place would we not take this as a preparation to launch an attack instead of suffer one, and in any case be tempted to attack sooner before the shelter program is completed? Or "safe" from accidental war or explosions? Will not the delusion of safety make precautions more lax while the threat and the tensions increase? Or "safe" from that large part of our "military-industrial complex" clamoring for a "war to prevent war"? What insanity that is!

Would it make anything "safe" for democracy? A lieutenant colonel, Chief of a Civil Defense Branch of the U.S. Army, stated to a group of Civil Defense leaders recently "Some civilians must be kept alive if only to feed us and give us bullets." If that was meant to be a joke, it isn't funny. The tragic reality is, however, that it would be true! With every third person dead or maimed, who — in these

4

proposed shelters — is going to care about free elections, civil rights and a constitution? How free would be those who are condemned to live in a poisoned world where sources of food and water are contaminated for years? The very callousness with which we are already turning human lives into statistics for determining policy mocks those "truths" which we once held self-evident "that all men are created equal, that they are endowed by their Creator with certain inalienable Rights, that among these are Life, Liberty and the Pursuit of Happiness. That to secure these rights Governments are instituted among men...." We feel this legislation endangers rather than secures these rights.

Finally, it is an alternative to something better. For every dollar and every man-hour spent on seeking imagined safety in existing buildings or ones to be constructed, there should be *ten* dollars and *ten* man-hours spent to make the use of shelters unnecessary. For every industry and research team like those which have testified today there should be *ten* subsidized by our government to put them out of work (with an honorable discharge, of course).

We, after all, *are* paying the bill for the colonel's food and bullets. But we are still his employers and not his slaves. We are willing to pay — in time, in money, in lives if necessary — whatever is needed to bring a better world for our children. But we will not gamble them for the miserable survival of a few in underground shelters. If we must gamble in this uncertain world, let us put everything we can toward the struggle for a better life for *all* our children *above the ground*. Let us redirect our aroused national energy and multiply our efforts to secure a just and workable peace!

"What are you—some kind of nut or something?"

ON THE OCCASION OF THE OPENING OF THE GENEVA DISARMAMENT CONFERENCE

With all the talk about preparing for nuclear war by building fallout shelters, the mere idea of "disarmament" seemed hopelessly utopian. Yet an international conference on the subject was scheduled in Geneva. Women for Peace held a rally in the bandstand at Golden Gate Park in San Francisco. I was elected to be the mistress of ceremonies, and I spoke again for the women.

Peace is no longer – in this nuclear age – a luxury to be enjoyed after our money is made, our jobs secure, our national pride satisfied, or our enemies exterminated. Peace is now a necessity to the survival of everything that is worth having: health, freedom, a tranquil mind, a secure future, a bounteous and beautiful land. It is necessary also to everything worth having about democracy: civil rights, respect for individuals, rule by law instead of force, and the right to participate in the decisions of the government.

Perhaps it is appropriate on the occasion of the Disarmament Conference to engage ourselves less in wishful sentiments for peace and more in realistic consideration of what we are prepared to pay individually and collectively in time, in money, in pride, in sovereignty. For, as Adlai Stevenson has said, "Let there be no mistake about it. General and complete disarmament envisages a degree of national self-restraint and of international intervention which is absolutely unprecedented." I think we can afford what we must afford: the alternative is hardly worth surviving for.

This talk was given in March, 1962, at the rally in San Francisco organized by Women for Peace.

7

If we stand firm on anything it should be, in my opinion, on the essentials of democracy: namely, the ultimate worth of persons, the rule of law, and participation by the people in the government. Life would be less worth living without these. But in all honesty we must remember that for 6000 years life was tolerable and sometimes even good without them. Nor is democracy necessarily the final achievement of political evolution. It may still be improved. Yet it is the best we have. I think we can stand firm on this, for the Russians too have everything to lose in war and much to gain in peace. Somewhere they must be saying "Better to be capitalist than decapitated." In fact, as they move economically toward free enterprise, and we toward government controls, we face the amusing prospect, we are told, of crossing past each other to opposite sides! Surely, then, we can get along politically without killing each other! So democracy is not, I think, the price of peace, and on this vital thing we can stand firm.

What then are we willing to pay? I think we could afford to pay, if asked, something of our standard of living. And we will be asked when the wartime economy is converted into a peacetime economy. I for one thing would be willing–even happy–to continue paying that 58% of my taxes that now goes to national defense toward re-employment of workers in productive, peacetime enterprises.

I think we could also give up some of our national pride. The game of "Keeping Ahead of the World" is harmless enough (though expensive) when played at the Olympics, in outer space, or at the conference table. But when it reaches the proportions of a national neurosis which would, in frantic and false pride, throw out all that is worthwhile about our country–civil rights, freedom to dissent, respect for law, and even the lives of 80 million of our men, women and children–the game has gone too far! The truly great can afford to be humble, and I would wish for my country that kind of greatness: not the kind that says "What is good for America is good for the world" but says "What is good for the world is good for America."

Further, it seems clear to me if we really want peace and disarmament, sooner or later we will have to give up a part of our national sovereignty and consent to be governed by a few world laws.

8

This we could afford without sacrificing the essentials of democracy, just as the thirteen colonies did in establishing the United States of America. The alternative of nuclear anarchy among the nations–five, then ten, then twenty-five of them–would be more devastating to democracy than any competing ideology.

The rule of law requires, according to John Locke, a "known and impartial judge," a "common superior on earth" which is recognized by all the partisans and has the power to enforce the law. Without this there would be anarchy or tyranny. Inspection of Americans or Russians on each other's territory could hardly be considered impartial judges. An International Disarmament Agency however, which is proposed by our negotiators to "verify the commitments of participating states" is a step in the right direction.

Another step is the inclusion for the first time in recent years of eight countries in this conference which are not connected with either the NATO or the Warsaw blocks. "This," as Stevenson says, "should serve to remind us that disarmament is not just a Great Power problem. The vast bulk of humanity is not disposed to accept, passively and wordlessly, the possibility of extermination without representation." This vast bulk of humanity may (and I think should) be that "common superior on earth" to which both the American and Russian protagonists must be willing to submit their cases.

In conclusion, I believe that, as people, we have more in common than in conflict with any group, that with the weapons now available war itself, rather than any group or nation, is the chief enemy of humanity, that the differences among us are not too great to be resolved if we show that we are reallly determined.

This is where we come in. In this country we, the people, are the masters, not servants of the government. We can speak therefore with more authority to our representatives in Geneva than can many other peoples. We are stronger too, when we are determined, than any pressure group which represents a special interest. We can speak out to our delegates and to the world in a voice that is clear and firm, and this is what I hope our voice will say:

- That we are in earnest about disarmament–general, complete, and to begin immediately:

9

- That we are growing impatient with fruitless talking and maneuvers while the arms race spirals out of control;
- That this race is no longer our game, nor is it in the interest of all the things we hold dear;
- That we are ready to join with the other peoples of the world in demanding a truce to the cold war, an end to the arms race, and the establishment of world order;
- That we are willing and can afford to pay whatever price we must in time, in money, in national pride and sovereignty for the accomplishment of a just, a practical plan for peace.

Our hope for disarmament is the hope of all humankind. Surely it is more basic than the special interests, investments and loyalties which divide us. As women, because we share the fundamental things: birth and growth, the nurture of life, the reality of pain, anxiety and death, we can and must unite with other women across artifical, man-made barriers to consummate our humanity in a world made safe for *people*. This is the hope, and I think the pledge of Women for Peace.

PREFACE TO THE WORRIED WOMAN'S GUIDE TO PEACE THROUGH WORLD LAW

As the women's movement grew, students and others joined in to protest the draft, the war weapons, the war in Vietnam, etc. One element that was missing in the movement, I thought, was attention to solutions or alternatives to war such as world law. So I collaborated with Esther Yudell of New York in writing the paperback titled, The Worried Woman's Guide to Peace Through World Law, *published in 1965 in the name of Women for Peace. The Preface is still mainly from the woman's point of view.*

     The time has come when the human family must find a way to live together. There is no longer anywhere to hide. Like it or not, we are being forced by circumstances to choose between anarchy among sovereign states, each with the power to destroy us all, and some kind of enforceable world order. Part of the circumstances are already upon us: the precarious situation inside the United Nations, with the Security Council immobilized by the veto and the Assembly disrupted by disagreement of the great powers over its authority in peacekeeping actions, China's emergence as a nuclear power outside the United Nations, and the temptation of smaller nations to follow the lead of Indonesia and break away from the United Nations –perhaps to set up a rival organization under China's leadership. Added to these are the devastation in Vietnam and the Congo, explosive conditions in the rest of S.E. Asia, Africa and South America (compounded by geometric increases in population), and the expansion of nuclear powers into outer space with the possibility, if uncontrolled, of asteroid bombs, orbiting H-bombs and irreversible contamination of this and other planets. The direction will be determined – and soon –

* Published in 1965 by Women for Peace

whether we take this awful road or a path to rational world government. Not to choose is to drift or be driven down that road.

No longer can we avoid with impunity the fundamental issue that must be faced on the path to peace: the institutional changes needed to secure "general and complete disarmament under effective international controls." We know that peace is not guaranteed by military alliances, threats of nuclear war, revolutions and vetoes. Nor can we rely on the theory of deterrence, that atomic version of "Si vir pacem, para bellum." It is unrealistic to sow thorns and expect a harvest of wheat. Such measures must be replaced as soon as possible with the rule of law, established under a constitution, with adequate powers delegated to enforce that law. In other words, the United Nations must be made into an effective world government.

Such a change, however, depends for its momentum on popular support for the ideal of a world community and some understanding of steps that need to be taken to achieve it. As individuals, many of us recognize that we have more in common than in conflict with people everywhere in the world. Loyalty to the basic human values of survival, health, and freedom for children to grow up in a wholesome environment is deeper (especially in women) than artificial abstractions of nationalism. Men and women can both contribute powerfully to the maturing of the world community by helping to create the attitudes and institutions which make it possible. This is the fundamental task of peace, and until we face it, all our efforts are stopgaps which cannot hope to meet the growing crises of rampant nationalism, for they treat only the symptoms and, at most, bring down the fever instead of curing the disease.

It is timely and vital for peacemakers to take a stand *now* for several reasons:

1. Many have protested their country's actions in Vietnam and elsewhere; constructive, long-range solutions should be sought, not just temporary alternatives to these actions.

2. The limitations of the United Nations have become increasingly apparent as its role in keeping the peace becomes more urgent. The inability to collect dues or to enforce decisions of the International

Court, the inequalities in representation, the veto power – these are but a few of the difficulties. U. Thant has pointed out that the United Nations is like a child being asked to take on man-sized problems. If in its present form it breaks down under the task, what will become of it, or what will take its place?

3. The year 1965 is the 20th anniversary of the United Nations; it is designated for review of the United Nations charter. It is also International Cooperation Year, a time for mobilizing the forces of peace to determine what kind of a world is wanted and the structure of government that will secure it.

4. For all of us it is time to spell out what is meant by "effective international controls" and what kind of peace we are working for. This could make a significant difference in the effectiveness of the peace movement as a constructive force in the world.

This book is intended for women *and men* who are worried about the condition of the world, who are weary of rushing from one stopgap measure to another while the danger increases. It is for those whose loyal disposition makes them tire of the role of tearing down old, false idols and yearn for the happier task of building the new day. Especially it is meant for those whose love of life is still deep and strong, uncorrupted by the global death-wish, potent enough to rise up with passion against the blasphemy of nuclear war and demand another way.

Then there would be a change in direction toward peace – a revolution, in fact – and that one could well be "women's work." (It has been said that mothers are the greatest revolutionary force in the world. When their instincts compel them to action they are irresistible. No one can long endure against them. Not the far right, the far left, or even that greatest enemy of revolution, the "extreme middle," can stand gracefully against motherhood defending its young.)

A revolution in human value such as this involves all people who are struggling for the dignity of the human being. There are many aspects to what is, essentially, the task of completing the democratic revolution by establishing the *people's* mastery over the political, economic and military institutions they have created. But the revolution needs a clearer focus, a more definite and more fundamental

13

objective. That must be the building of a structure within which the human family can live, play, work, and quarrel together without destroying each other's rights. A worldwide institution in which general and complete disarmament can be achieved "under effective international controls" is essential to the survival of the human race. A democratic form of world government in which people rule themselves through representatives of their own choosing and laws of their own making is essential to their dignity and freedom. Achievements of these objectives – soon – is the condition on which all other objectives depend: Negro rights, civil liberties, economic security, mental and physical health ...

The only alternative to war is law – until we all become saints, and that will be a long time! If fear of sudden nuclear war would only induce us to re-read history, "We would see how wars were stopped between families, tribes, feudal barons, municipalities, principalities and other units that were battling each other. Those wars ceased forever when the warring sovereign units were integrated into a higher legal order." (Emery Reves in *The Anatomy of Peace*)

Creating such an order is a difficult task, and its intricacies can perhaps be left to experts. The general design, however, is the concern of everyone, especially of women, who have made homes and communities for their families and can tell what serves best the human need. To outline the shape of a world community that will provide a good environment for its people – this is women's work as well as men's.

The first step is to be informed. Three blueprints have been presented for changing the United Nations into an organization that would better fit our present needs: *first,* strengthening the United Nations by revision of the UN Charter, which would be like shoring up the foundations of a building and patching the roof; *second,* establishing an additional agency within the framework of the United Nations called "World Disarmament and World Development Organization" by a separate treaty among nations, which would be like building an annex; *and third,* calling a constitutional convention for drafting a world constitution, which would be like starting again at the foundations. Which of these plans (or some other) is the wisest? We must decide soon, or it will be too late.

Then we must act by every means available, through individual effort and organizations, to effect the needed change. Nothing could be more important *–ever–* to the survival of the human race!

Time is running out. We dare not waste it now in petty bickering or lame excuses: "War is human nature." "Nations would never give up their sovereignty." "Would you want your daughter to ...?" "Look at the 'backward nations' – can't even govern themselves!" "Governments are too big already." "World tyranny – that's what!" "You can't trust the Communists." "The world isn't ready for it." "Don't rock the boat." "It won't work."

We've heard all this before. No one demands a guarantee before starting a war. Billions of dollars and lives are spent – for what? Yet, when it comes to building the essential institutions of peace, impossible guarantees are demanded, improbable consequences imagined, so that nothing is done and a point of total paralysis is reached. Those brave few who are already working against such odds need us *now*. Let us say what women have said to their men from the beginning of time, "What *must* be done *shall* be done. That's all that counts. *Let's get going!"*

Logo of the World Constitution and Parliament Association

REFLECTIONS ON THE FIRST WORLD CONSTITUTIONAL CONVENTION

But women did not take to long-range abstractions such as world law & world government (nor did the peace movement, for that matter), and I became involved with what seemed to me more constructive solutions. Responding to another "Call," I participated in the "Preparatory Congress for a World Constitutional Convention" in Denver, Colorado in 1963 and the first "World Constitutional Convention" in Switzerland in 1968. This emotional account reflects both the highs and lows of this experience. (I was in Interlaken the week when Russian tanks rolled into Czechoslovakia, which prevented a number of Czechs and other East Europeans from attending the Convention.)

In a country of mountains a milestone seems very small. And so it did that Sunday, August 25th, looking down from the still, blue-and-white summit of the Jungfrau along miles of glacier inching imperceptibly toward a different world—far below—of tumbling waters feeding a land of many hues. Time and space were poised as in a snapshot. Could this be the moment so many had prepared for over the last ten years, hoping it would be a turning point toward peace?

Four hours later the desk clerk at my hotel greeted me back with news that someone had arrived from France and was asking for me. It had started! Over the next two days a hundred and fifty people arrived from thirty countries, including Ceylon, India, Pakistan, Thailand, Kenya, Nigeria, Ghana, Norway, Finland, Israel, and from as far away as Brazil, Colombia and Peru. Dozens came from France, England, Germany and Switzerland, and finally, in a torrent of rain, tired and disheveled from a grueling trip, the U.S. contingent of thirty-five arrived ten minutes late for the opening ceremonies.

For the remainder of that week in Interlaken and the following ten days in Wolfach, Germany, a rigorous schedule of meetings continued from 9 a.m. to 10 p.m., and often at friendly beerhalls into the early morning hours. World citizens from five continents, from

17

every major religion, every color, from rich and poor countries, old and young–all worked and played together, demonstrating in operation what they proposed to establish into law: that people are essentially of one family whose country is the whole world. This, despite the grim headlines of invasion in Czechoslovakia and riots in Chicago!

By the end of the first week of speeches, planning and debate, the members approved unanimously the first proposal for action, the creation of an "Institute for Research and Documentation on World Federal Authority" as a means to secure the participation of national governments. Although the vote was unanimous, it was evident from the discussion that a divergence already existed between those who wished to work through established institutions and those who felt the need of a radical shift of allegiance. For the moment the policy prevailed of "everyone to his own way," and the Institute was endorsed with encouragement for its implementation.

By now delegates were eager for more action, and it came. We moved as planned to Wolfach, a world-city in the black forest of southwest Germany. The reception there was very friendly. During all the days of our convention the U.N. flag flew on the city hall, together with the dark blue flag of the Council of Europe loaned by that body for the occasion. The village was quiet, but its inhabitants pleasant, the beer good and the moon full–and so work went on day and night. We divided into eight commissions for drafting a constitution and proposals for action. Three proposals were adopted and will go forward, one action was rejected, and the four dealing with a constitution, general views and basic principles to be embodied were put into the record for consideration in future working sessions in 1969 and 1970.

One of the three projects that will go forward is a World University. It will attempt to develop coordination among the many educational projects already applying a world perspective, establish a post-graduate school directed toward studying problems with an eye to world needs, and thereby produce persons uniquely competent to staff and advise international organizations, both governmental and non-governmental. Upon acceptance, this proposal was taken by

18

Professor Alfred Kastler to the ensuing UNESCO conference in Paris for their advice and support. An international board was formed, including many of those who had worked with the commission in Wolfach, with Mr. H.K.M. Defares of The Netherlands as chairman. The World Academy of Art and Science was to be contacted, and an offer of land and money for such an enterprise was to be investigated.

A second program adopted (way ahead of its time) was in ecology and conservation. It was grounded in aesthetic and moral principles as well as practical concern for the future of the human race. Aiming at preserving a normal balance between humans and their environment, now disturbed by the explosions in population and technology, it asserted the necessity of planning the size of population in accordance with natural resources available and, further, that "the elements of life–earth, water, air and energy–are the common heritage of the human race and shall be managed for "the common good of this and future generations." Recognizing the responsibility of people for all living creatures, principles were included of the International Society for the Protection of Animals to insure humane conditions for domestic and captive animals and to eliminate cruelty and suffering inflicted by humans whether in the interests of science, sport, entertainment or the production of food.

An agency was proposed for administering the program as part of a "world authority" when established. A cooperative corporation was suggested with members functioning for the benefit of all people , which would act as trustee for future world parks, territories and oceans.

A third project came out of the Commission on Communication, namely, the creation of a four-page, world-wide newspaper to be published monthly under the name "Man" to serve world government and peace movements. Mr. and Mrs. Arthur Brackman of New York would undertake this with the help of other members of the commission and of business and professional people from other countries among delegates to the convention.

Disagreement broke out again over the method of political action to be pursued until the next convention in 1970. The Political Action Commission (made up largely of younger "activists" from western nations) proposed an Emergency World Government of recognized leaders to be proclaimed as an authority which individuals would be called on to acknowledge voluntarily, superseding national authority only in critical issues of survival, and to be superseded itself within a stated time by a democratic world government. This proposition contradicted the views of some delegates from Asia and the developing countries, who looked on their governments as the best instruments for achieving freedom, world government and peace. The breach, understandable though unexpected as it was, resulted in the proposal being rejected as an action by the convention. However, the commission promptly re-formed itself as an independent group to pursue the project on its own with Mrs. Garry Davis as General Secretary.

So what did that leave for political action by other delegates to the convention? Clearly, they would continue in their different ways to carry out their responsibilities to their constituencies and to increase the latter, so that the 1970 convention would represent more than 120,000 people. As evidence of determination to follow through, an office was opened in San Francisco by California delegates and supporters. From here (in San Francisco) the mountain peak in Switzerland seems far away, yet something has happened in between— an event, clear and irreversible, a milestone between plan and action on the road to a world community.

---

* Note: This convention was organized by the World Constitution & Parliament Assocation of Denver, Colorado. It has been followed by a series of conventions resulting, among other things, in the creation and adoption of *A Constitution for the Federation of Earth*.

FROM TERRITORIAL TO ECOLOGICAL IMPERATIVE

I was one of the first to recognize the importance of environmental issues to survival on this planet. In 1968 I had been Chairperson of the Ecology Commission at the WCC in Switzerland because I was the only one who could define the term, "ecology." (I had just learned it from a student at Merritt College, who later became the founder of Ecology Action.) I anticipated the concern over the oceans with a conference in Berkeley on "Two-thirds of the World Up for Grabs" in 1969, and also the eventual convergence of peace and ecology movements for survival. This philosophical article is reminiscent of my earlier ideas on education–with an added dimension.

Ecology today describes a world-wide movement of thought and action that is profoundly revolutionary. Now that the first skirmishes are over (1975) the dust is clearing on the lines of conflict, and the issues can be more clearly defined in basic metaphysical and moral terms. It is just possible that herein lies a deeper understanding of what the revolution is *really* about and why it is necessary.

Moral values are produced by a combination of rational necessity (enlightened self-interest) and "consciousness" (expressed as compassion or empathy). These two forces have converged under the banner of Ecology for the survival of the human species and the various forms of nature with which its fate is interwoven. Simple intelligence is required, with only a *little* foresight, to understand the catastrophe that lies in the direction of present trends. The collision course of people and nature has been amply pointed out by authorities on population, energy, and food resources. It is becoming increasingly apparent to informed laymen that their destiny is linked with an

---

* First published in UNIQUEST, 1st Unitarian Church of Berkeley, 1975

intricate balance of water, air, earth and energy, and that this balance also involves plants and animals, as well as other human beings.

At the same time an unprecedented network of audio-visual "empathy machines" has brought the marvels and idiosyncracies of nature into the living room, stimulating the imagination and emotions to new levels of consciousness. Never has there been more intimate exposure to the "secrets" of nature, nor to its amazing achievements. Thus, the doomsday prophesies, together with a heightened appreciation of the complexity of life, combine to forge a new shape for morality out of necessity to consider the total environment. The obligation derived from this necessity is "The Ecological Imperative,"– that is, the duty to act out of respect for the *total environment*.

Axioms

The new morality recognizes and accepts as a first axiom the dynamic interdependence of nature. The environment is viewed as an organic system in which human, animal and plant life interact with one another as well as with water, air, earth and energy (the so-called "inert" material systems) in a synergy of process. This interaction is intricate and often unpredictable, like a living organism many of whose variables cannot be measured in chemical or physical terms: potential, inventiveness, self-determination, will, spirit. As in a living organism, damage to one vital system may cause malfunctions in related systems, even "death" of the whole organism, as has been discovered (hopefully in time) in the ecosystems of lakes, rivers and the oceans. Ecosystems do not work like machines, which can be "fixed" by taking out any unit, tinkering with it and putting it back again – not if that "unit" is an extinguished species of life.

Another axiom of the new morality is that environment is multi-dimensional. The many interdependent systems operate in different dimensions of space, time, motion and consciousness. Even "material" systems (water, air, earth, and energy) which follow the laws of chemistry and physics, differ in their dimensions. Earth is only two-dimensional and the most tractable of all. It is the *only* one of the four systems that can be "zoned," the basis of the so-called "Territorial Imperative" to which Robert Ardrey ascribes motives of animals and men. In the past, most people's values–material, political

22

and social–have been built on the "necessity" of possessing and defending pieces of land. However, it is now clear that air, water and energy submit to no such "territorial imperative." They cannot be zoned, because they operate in dimensions that cannot be fenced in or walled off. They are not static. And yet the real value of land depends on its relation to these dynamic systems which cannot be "territorialized." It took pollution and an energy crisis to show that zoning of feeding grounds, farming areas, cities and nation-states must be replaced by a multi-dimensional approach to the earth's resources. If the land is to sustain life, it must harmonize with water, air and energy; and these, like the sun, cannot be bounded. The two- and three-dimensional world of the materialistic perspective becomes multi-dimensional in the ecological perspective. It is as impossible to define the latter in territorial measurements as it is to explain color in black and white.

Furthermore, the environment takes on more dimensions with each rise in the level of consciousness. The mass media, and also the fact that things seem more valuable as they are less taken for granted, heighten our concern over endangered species of animals, plants and wilderness areas. These forms of life suddenly appear to have intrinsic, aesthetic value as things of beauty, even moral value as subjects-in-themselves. They have become, to people who care, "beings" worthy of admiration and respect, rather than "things" to be disposed of at will, for whatever trivial whim, sport or fashion. Conservationists who rise to the defense of wildlife, redwoods, scenic shorelines and whales are moved by growing sensitivity and compassion. They arrive too late, alas, for hundreds of species. Yet they demonstrate a new awareness of the beauty, intricacy, and astonishing order in the balance of nature, so long in the making and so vulnerable to myopic man. The higher levels of consciousness perceive more and more life-systems to be *subjects* rather than *objects,* lying within the "I-Thou" relation rather than the "I-it" (including, it should be noted, other *humans* like minorities, women, and strangers). The process is not complete, but the direction is clear: the principle of the Golden Rule must extend to man's treatment of all sentient life, and the maxim that will become the universal law of the ecological imperative will be "Reverence for Life."

A third axiom of the new morality is the duty to measure actions in relation to the *future* as well as to the past and present. Persons today have a moral obligation to refrain from self-indulgence so that future generations can have a decent standard of living. We are faced with the problem of "loving our neighbors" who are living in the future. The commitment to a future liveable world requires stretching both moral faculties–reason and compassion–to a degree without precedent. Is it expecting too much of humanity to make such a commitment? Our hope lies, if at all, in a deep, as yet untapped reservoir of commitment to life's continuance. We need to cultivate a future dimension to duty. Imagine "I-Thou" becoming the *moral* relation to those yet unborn!

Mature Virtues

The ecological imperative will demand a higher priority than in the past for mature virtues such as caution, prudence and frugality which, during the years of experimental technology, have been subordinated to such youthful virtues as courage, curiosity and exuberance. To try anything until you find a reason not to may have been admired in times when mistakes could be corrected, but is indefensible in times of nuclear fission and genetic engineering with potentials for irreversible damage to the environment. The world, regarded as a living organism, must be treated with the respect of a doctor for his patient; when mistakes are irreversible, the virtue is to *not do anything* unless you have a *very* good reason. Caution and prudence are demanded in a physician, along with knowledge, skill, and wisdom. Courage and curiosity are rarely admired in a person who holds in his hand the balance of life and death! Some mistakes in judgment undoubtedly will be made in spite of everything, but they can be minimized by a code of ethics consistent with the ecological imperative. A precedent has been set by the geneticists who met recently at Asilomar and pledged restraint in their research, moving to set "fail-safe" conditions for hybrid DNA experiments.

The good life and the good society of the future will not be the materialistic joyride of the past, but will have to be defined in new terms compatible with a balanced ecosystem.

We have been two-dimensional creatures in a multi-dimensional world which cannot be forced into a perspective that is flat, material, and present-oriented. We are in danger of toppling the delicate, many-faceted experiments in life which have evolved over billions of years. The direction and momentum is clear, and no one today can plead ignorance. "Father, forgive them not, for they know what they do" will be said of our generation. It is an awesome responsibility for one generation of one of *millions* of species to wield such power over the evolution of life! Even if we do nothing, the chances are that much, if not all, of life will be destroyed, for the forces are already in motion: nuclear and biological weapons *alone* could do it hundreds of times over in the "defense" of imagined national (territorial) "interests."

Our generation can choose to assist at a *new* experiment in conscious and deliberate cultivation of a safer, healthier environment for all living things on earth. Perhaps we are not wise enough – yet. But we can change, for that is the way life has survived in the past. Fortunately, ideas can change quickly when reason and consciousness perceive the necessity. We need only to raise our sights from a myopic view of nature and man to the multi-dimensional view of the ecological imperative. And then? Who knows what other dimensions lie beyond–in outer space and inner space – what forms of consciousness and life higher than man's may be evolved, discovered or created? We know little of the limits of space, of intelligence, of sensitivity, of morality. The limits may well be only limits of our imagination, not of the capacity of life. If life continues, with a little help from us, future dimensions of being may be as far beyond our present understanding as consciousness is beyond the comprehension of inert, three-dimensional matter.

We can at least keep the experiment going!

PART II

THE HIGH ROAD AND
THE LOW ROAD

THE LOW ROAD TO WORLD LAW

By 1974 confidence was waning in the ability of national governments, elected officials, or "decision-makers in and out of government (the "high road") to create a peaceful world. This reflected on the United Nations, which is an organization of nation states (in spite of its Charter's opening with "We the People"). Hope for the future is here transferred to the growing movement of people throughout the world protesting that their needs are not being met. They are, in fact, victims of war and the arms race. This movement I called the "Low Road" to peace.

"He who would really fight for justice must do so as a private citizen, not as a political figure." So said Socrates 2,400 years ago. Today, as we watch the repeated frustration of efforts to create a viable world organization by revision of the U.N. Charter, we do well to remember these words. For it is from the private quarter, it seems to me, that the impetus for a world community must now come. After all, it is the PEOPLE who want and need peace; it is the governments that wage wars. Eisenhower once said, "The people want peace so badly that governments should get out of their way and let them have it." They should, but of course they won't.

Current efforts to get the nations which constitute the U.N. to reform its charter, to establish and operate an effective environmental agency and create an international ocean regime, despite agreements they may have along the way, all run into the same roadblock. As Harry Reasoner said of the Moscow and Peking summit meetings, "The dirty word is still there, and the word is 'sovereignty.' Sovereignty is a word which, in affairs between tribes and nations, means that tribes or nations can do anything they want to....What it means is that the papers signed in Moscow with such great hope and sincerity by Breshnev and Nixon could be abrogated next year by two new

27

leaders who felt differently or by the same men if circumstances changed. They would need no reason except the right of sovereign states to raise hell and there is no superogatory power around to even give them a parking ticket." (ABC News, May 30, 1972)

Attempts to move the Establishment toward an effective world administration have not been lacking in prestige. They have had money, leadership, public relations experts and the support of many distinguished and competent world figures. Yet, twenty-nine years after the founding of the U.N., they can point to only minor advances, like the increase in size of the Security Council. Little or no progress has been made toward the essentials of world government: disarmament, effective peacekeeping machinery, financial security for the U.N., a world court. Why has so little been accomplished by so much?

One reason is growing apparent: NATIONS WILL NOT TRANSFER THEIR OWN SOVEREIGNTY. No nation state is willing–or even able–to transfer its power to some other agent; nor is its representative, whether appointed or elected, in a position to do other than protect the special interests of that nation, whatever his personal views may be. It is unreasonable, as well as clearly ineffectual to press him to do so. He is not free, but bound by duty to his country.

On the contrary, nations, in a desperate effort to fulfill their "obligations," are drawn into a deadly game of "Chicken" by the advancing technology of weapons. It is dawning on people that their interests are no longer served by their governments pursuing this game. Even if they could "win," it is too costly and too dangerous. In the madness of staying "ahead" in the race, the guardian-state is transmuted into an all-consuming Frankenstein monster, while real needs of real people for decent homes, health, education, security are eclipsed by the chimera of national power.

Even the United Nations, "the last, best hope of peace," is still part of that game. As its name implies, it is an association of nations, not of people. As long as nations retain ultimate power the only possible relation among them is a voluntary assembly. They are, in fact, a confederation of sovereign states like the thirteen American colonies under the Articles of 1776. Representatives to the United Nations are "ambassadors" of de facto governments, representing the policy of the administration rather than the will of the people. Thus, the U.S. Ambassador is a representative of the President, not his party, the Congress, or the people. There is no way the opposition on any issues–say the Cambodia policy–can be presented to the U.N. Assembly, even if it happens to represent the majority of the people! In some countries the administration even makes no pretense of democratically reflecting its "constituency." As long as this is so, the Security Council and the Assembly of the U.N. comprising the political forum of the world, must remain little more than arenas for power politics.

The people, themselves, must bring the governments "to heel." But how?

Some observations from United States history are suggestive. The call to re-draft the Articles of Confederation was originated – not by Congress or one of the states–but by the small group of "delegates" from five states which met at Annapolis in 1786. They took the initiative when it was clear that the Articles of Confederation, like the United Nations Charter, were inadequate to the task required of them. And the men who met in Philadelphia in 1787 weren't authorized to draw up a new constitution. They went to make a few amendments to the Articles of Confederation. But they came to the conclusion– most of them–that newer, bolder plans were needed. Their work was authenticated after it was done, not before.

Some efforts by private world citizens have been building across national barriers the structure of a democratic organization to represent people of the world, rather than their governments. In 1968, for example, two hundred individuals from five continents, many of them representing constituencies of 1000 or more people, met in a "Constitutional Convention" and "Peoples World Parliament" in Switzerland. This was part of an ongoing movement to establish a democratic world government by a grass-roots initiative. In January 1972, a similar group met in Santa Barbara, California, calling itself

29

an "Emergency Council of World Trustees." Progress was made there involving a large number of student body leaders to prepare for a permanent, ongoing nucleus for a Peoples World Parliament and a tentative World Constitution. Agreement was also reached among the 70+ Trustees from 19 countries on a First Decree for the Protection of Life, a Population and Ecology Program, and other documents charting a course of action toward a world organized to "put human priorities first."

In 1975, thirty years after the founding of the United Nations in San Francisco, an assembly of world citizens will be held in that same city to further advance the grass roots effectiveness of people acting together across national barriers for their own survival and dignity, and to build a world community.

Such actions do not make headlines—even have difficulty making the newspapers —and are lacking in money and prestige that have been lavished upon the attempts to move the Establishment along the High Road to world law. Yet, barring some miracle, military conquest, or disaster that might transform the sovereign states, this Low Road, it seems to me, is the safer, more logical, more promising path to peace.

THE UNITED NATIONS:
WHERE DO WE GO FROM HERE?

As the arms race accelerated and human needs went unmet, specific problems of the United Nations became more apparent. Proposals for U.N. reform were advanced, but there was no support for the fundamental structural change needed to make the U.N. work. I picture the U.N. here as a stage in an unfinished process moving towards a governed world. Parallels to U.S. history in the 18th century are suggested.

Four billion years it took for natural evolution to achieve, by trial and error, the world of which we are a part. The last four thousand of these years could be called "conscious evolution," the tiny fraction of time that has been recorded in history, still shaped largely by trial and error. In the last forty years deliberate, planned evolution has become possible. The Germans began in the 1930's to apply a plan using genetic and military science. At the end of the war the explosion of the atomic bomb multiplied the possibilities for changing deliberately the course of evolution. Alarmed at the existence of power with such awesome consequences, forty-eight nations, constituting most of the existing powers of that time, came together in San Francisco in 1945 to form the United Nations "to save succeeding generations from the scourge of war..." Its founding is a milestone on the way to intelligent, collective planning for the future of this planet.

The accomplishments of the United Nations in the years of its existence have been many:
- a permanent forum for the nations of the world
- consensus on certain humane principles, spelled out in the Charter and Declaration of Human Rights

---

* Based on a talk presented October 23rd, 1977, "U.N. Sunday" at The First Unitarian Church, Berkeley, California and reprinted in *Political World Union,* the Netherlands in June, 1978; and with some revisions in *Dhama World,* Tokyo, Japan, March, 1980.

- regulation of the airways, postal service and other international traffic
- humanitarian agencies such as FAO, WHO, UNICEF
- a series of world conferences on the environment, food, population, habitat, oceans, which have produced intelligent, even noble statements of principle and conscience
- a tripling in membership with increased representation and support, especially among the developing countries

The United Nations is truly a milestone in "deliberate evolution" toward a civilized world.

Ironically, one of the greatest dangers today may be that we think we have "arrived." We still have a long way to go; there is not much time, and the hazards are growing. Since the United Nations has been in existence there have been increasing signs that things are getting out of control: the population explosion, famine, pollution, a widening gap between rich and poor, crime and terrorism on the rise. We are told that we have the technology to solve our problems, yet they get worse, and money that could be used for solving them is sucked up into a whirlwind of armaments and profits. Why? Because present structures cannot get at the basic cause of disorder, and continue instead to treat only the symptoms with partial remedies. It is like treating cancer with bandaids and aspirin. The CAUSE is unlimited power — enough to destroy four billion years of growth — wielded by institutions with myopic perspectives and tribal or commercial values. The independent, sovereign nation-state, which is the form of government established by territorial imperative in the last two hundred years, is based on self-determination and military force. Unfortunately, this form of independence, the sovereign nation, is the form of government institutionalized in the United Nations.

There are, of course, other forms of power: rich individuals, scientists, economic classes (including labor), corporations, the press. These may also in some cases be unchecked by rational, humane or altruistic constraints. But there is no area of life where it is more urgent to set limits than in that of national sovereignty. For here the new technologies of military and psychological warfare have created the deadliest power — deliberate, calculating, malignant. Like a cancer, it is eating away at the vital core of civilization (including the United Nations), a threat to every hard-won liberty and human dignity, to every rational balance between freedom and order. Before it, all other issues pale, and many situations that are already intolerable cannot be remedied until this cancer is checked. Yet, somehow we have come to accept this monstrous condition as bearable — to tolerate the intolerable! And we look blindly to what has been called "the last, best hope of peace," which is actually an assembly of these sovereign states which wield unlimited powers.

We have learned how to limit the sovereign power of the state in internal affairs. Through centuries of struggle, sacrifice and experiment a constitutional form of government with bill of rights has been brought forth in a few western countries, limiting the power of ruler over subject by a "social contract" which binds both to certain agreed-on conditions put in writing. This remarkable device can be traced symbolically to the first "contract" God made with Noah, agreeing never again to destroy the earth by flood. The signature on that contract was — and still is — the rainbow! Covenants followed with Abraham and with Moses. Later, when earthly kings were less inclined to voluntary self-limitation than the God of Noah, contracts were imposed on them by necessity, as the Magna Carta was on King John and the Bill of Rights of 1688 on William of Orange. The American and French constitutions followed with a Bill of Rights, spelling out that Congress shall make NO laws abridging freedom of speech, religion and the press . These internal limits to the power of the state over the individual have worked out reasonably well where applied, and are probably still acceptable to most people as limits to government's freedom within the state.

But there are NO SUCH LIMITS on national sovereignty outside the state! Between and among the nations there are no checks on the freedom to act except the intolerance of other nations, backed by force. Thus a "balance of terror" is created which causes the arms race and proliferation of nuclear weapons. The United Nations cannot cope with such threats to global survival. For the United Nations does not represent the world, or the people in it, or any form of world community. It reflects, quite realistically, the existing "balance of terror," especially among the big powers. It also gives, quite unrealistically, an equal vote to every member nation in the Assembly without regard to size, population, wealth or power. At the same time each country vehemently maintains its "sovereign right" to determine the size and deployment of its military, its population, its pollution, its exploitation of natural resources. Any achievements for the common good are due to overlapping self-interests — and there are some, of course, which we have cited, in non-military, non-political areas. But as an instrument for managing the earth's affairs the United Nations is structurally flawed. As "the last, best hope of peace" it is not promising. The problems of an interdependent world cannot be managed by an assemblage of independent principalities. The common good of all should not be limited by the special interest of any one section of the earth's surface, no matter how large, or rich, or powerful. Rather, the special interest of each one must be limited by the common good.

By any rational standard (and even by the so-called "territorial imperative") the "sovereign right" of nations does not extend beyond its territorial boundaries. It should be limited to internal affairs. The anarchy now existing in inter-national affairs must be replaced by supra-national institutions with a global perspective.

The view of the world as seen from space is "a beautiful blue planet," not a patchwork of pink, yellow and purple blotches separated by dotted lines. A wholistic, one-world view is emerging from space travel and other miracles of modern technology and from communication. A new consciousness is also emerging from a growing awareness in the West of the wisdom of the Eastern world-view. Buddhism, Hinduism, Taoism and Shinto, while they differ in many respects, portray the world as a multi-dimensional, organically interrelated eco-system of which man is one of many inter-dependent parts. Perhaps we can learn through them to see the world whole, as it really is, and together — West and East — begin to build the foundations of a new world order.

The most urgent item on the planetary agenda is to set the limits of freedom and order in supra-national, global affairs. A constitution for the world is needed which combines the achievements of both hemispheres: that is, constitutional limitations and a bill of rights from the West and a spacious world-view from the East. Principles such as the following would be incorporated:

- human dignity, the intrinsic value of every human life
- reverence for all life: plant, animal and human
- ecological balance among the many-dimensional systems of nature
- subordination of special interests to the common good
- certain inalienable rights for all people
- a "known and written law," government by contract, not arbitrary force

Just as the U.S. Constitution, with Declaration of Independence, established the patterns for national independence and personal liberty so important in the last two hundred years, so a constitution with a Declaration of *Inter*dependence, could establish patterns of interdependence and personal responsibility needed now and for the future.* Whether the transformation can best be made by changing the United Nations through revision of its Charter or by bypassing it and starting again from the grass roots, is a matter of debate over strategy. In contrast to the former method, which is somewhat like asking a person to operate on his own cancer, there is NOTHING in the way of direct action by the people except apathy due to lack of faith and

---

NOTE: * Based essentially on these East-West principles of interdependence, A Constitution for the Federation of Earth has been completed, after ten years' work by people from two dozen countries and all five continents, and signed by 160 participants at an assembly of world citizens in Innsbruck, Austria in June, 1977. This is another important milestone in conscious, deliberate evolution toward a world community. It brings the new world order down from the skies onto the drawing boards, and even proposes a step-by-step plan of action to achieve it. A three-house World Parliament is proposed, one house constituting a federation of nations (the United Nations transformed from a confederation of independent states to a federation as done in the United States in 1789). Another house would be elected by and responsible directly to the people of the world, who by nature have more in common than their countries, and a third "House of Counsellors" elected from people nominated for their ability "to represent the highest good and best interest of humanity as a whole."

Copies of the Constitution may be obtained by writing to World Constitution and Parliament Association, 1480 Hoyt St., Suite 31, Lakewood, Colorado 80215, U.S.A. ($5)

nerve! This is sad when the knowledge and instruments are so nearly at hand!

Perhaps it is our affluence that makes us apathetic. There's something about being well-off and reasonably secure that does not inspire courage and commitment, even when reason commands it. It is well to remember that two-thirds of the world is not thus afflicted by affluence, and is therefore determined to have change, no matter how it is brought about. Each of us who luxuriates in leisurely programs of "self-realization" does so at the tolerance of intolerable conditions of survival by most of the people in the world. This cannot — will not last!

As human beings gifted with the ability to see ahead as well as behind, with the ability to stand and look up to the stars as well as in to ourselves; as a favored part of the human species in our comparative security and wealth and in all the instruments for peaceful change at our command; as a fellowship of people committed to the use of reason, non-violence and love in the creation of a world community, let us move with courage and faith — and more appropriate urgency — to secure, by conscious and deliberate effort, the future of this lovely planet, a heritage of four billion years entrusted to humankind.

NEEDED: A PERMANENT PEOPLES ASSEMBLY

In June, 1978 at the first United Nations Special Session on disarmament I was involved, with Dr. Harry Lerner of New York, in the organization of a Peoples Assembly. It was a public forum, meeting across the street from the U.N. to discuss the same issues from a "peoples" perspective. There were exchanges with speakers from the U.N., as well as authorities in various fields related to disarmament. Resolutions from the Peoples Assembly were sent to the U.N. at the end of the five-week session. The dismal results of the deliberations inside the U.N., which I called the "battle of the brackets" inspired the conclusion in this speech, and the vision of an eventual peoples house incorporated into a democratized U.N. structure.

After five strenuous weeks of intense effort by thousands of people both in and out of governments — most of whom are informed, intelligent and well-intentioned, there is no solution in sight to the problem of disarmament. The one thing that seems clear is that the facts of the arms race are utterly appalling — beyond the limited capacity of human imagination to comprehend, though not beyond the unlimited capacity of human ingenuity to produce, in a world gone mad with inter-necine rivalry between competitive national systems. Facts have been repeated ad nauseum about the overkill, about new, more terrible weapons on the drawing boards, about the escalation of nuclear and conventional weapons in countries both rich and poor, about the increasing burden in taxes, and about all the unmet needs that could be met by reversing the arms race. The facts point clearly to a world gone mad, and yet sane, gentle people have spent 35 days deliberating this intolerable situation in the United Nations, mostly involved in a Battle of the Brackets among representatives of the very

---

* A talk given in New York after the first Special U.N. Session on Disarmament in July, 1978.

nations engaged in the arms race. Other sane, gentle people outside of the U.N. have cheered them on and talked endlessly about facts and figures and the need for "general and complete disarmament." The most that could be expected from this massive effort is a tenuous "Declaration of Principles" and an agreement to resume deliberations in three years! Meanwhile, the race goes on to see which nation can get closest to the precipice without falling over — and taking all the other nations with it, not to mention all the people and other living things which, after four billion years of evolution, would be brought to an end.

The only sane thing to do in a no-win game is to change the game. And the game of competing nations is NOT the only game in town, contrary to those in the cheering section who take satisfaction in watching the game and hoping against hope for some happy resolution. The time has come to recognize that IT'S THE WRONG GAME TO PLAY in this modern, interdependent world. There is a structural flaw in the present system of trying to manage the world's security and other problems by means of independent national states. Nations are the product of an age of frontiers, of limited horizons and limited technologies. They are structurally incapable of managing the affairs of a world in which frontiers are meaningless because of developments in technology and communications, and in which interdependent systems of human and ecological problems need to be solved.

What is needed is an institution to represent the common interests of people regardless of national identity — the needs for survival and security, which their own nations canNOT provide, and for food, housing, jobs and other human rights that could be guaranteed if the arms race were disengaged. The Non-Governmental Organizations could be the founders of such an institution if they would remove themselves from the cheering section. Many of them are larger in sheer numbers of people represented than most of the nations now in the U.N. Furthermore, most of them are supra-national in scope and are functional (i.e. service-oriented) in nature. They are therefore complementary rather than competitive, and it is conceivable that together they could be cooperative, representative and responsible to a global constitency of people and other living things, that up to now have been the tragic victims in a game of "Chicken." Whether the leaders of NGO's that have been accredited by the United Nations as "observers" or "consultants" can take on this much stronger role remains to be seen.

Meanwhile, the Peoples Assembly, an independent body open to all NGO's, accredited or not, and to concerned individuals as well, met throughout the Special Session on Disarmament. It will continue as a precedent and possible nucleus for forming a truly global institution to represent the common interests of people rather than the competing interests of nations. A Peoples Assembly will be held every time and place the U.N. special sessions are held on problems that concern people in general, such as the future of the oceans, technology, and childrens rights. The Peoples Assembly should be financed by the proposed "disarmament tax" if possible, and by grants and individual contributions if necessary, until it is soundly incorporated into the structure of the U.N. as a permanent house — a Peoples Assembly with the voting power to change the no-win game of disunited nations into an all-win game for enhancement of life on this planet.

Dr. Lucile W. Green is Professor of Philosophy & Humanities, President of World Citizens Assembly and Co-Convenor with Dr. Harry Lerner of New York of the Peoples Assembly for the SSD.

Logos of the International Cooperation Council,
World Citizens, Federalist Caucus and World
Federalist Association.

40

CONVERGENCE: THE HIGH ROAD AND THE LOW ROAD

In a poetic mood reflecting probably my Taoist orientation, I use the metaphor of converging rivulets merging ultimately in a rushing river of change. Temporarily blocked by man-made constructs of language, territoriality, power trips and communication problems, the flow of life-forces in the peace and environment movements is sluggish—a marshy network, but with the potential of breaking loose. In retrospect, it seems to anticipate the torrent of change toward "democracy" released by the thaw in the cold war in the late '80's.

The way of life is to flow. Like water originating in pure mountain springs, it trickles down through natural channels into streams which, fed by many sources, increase until they converge into mighty rivers which flow at last into the vast ocean. This "ocean" is not uniform, as it appears on the surface, but contains an infinite variety of species interrelating in a common environment. There is something natural and inevitable about the flow of water to the sea. In spite of diversions, meanderings, being dammed up, or polluted or dissipated, it eventually somehow reaches the ocean.

The way of humans, on the other hand, is to build. Since our emergence out of innocence, symbolized by the Garden of Eden, we have had to deal with a world fractured by language into particles — nouns, verbs, adjectives — which we must reconstruct into the forms by which we order our lives. In our arts — language arts, visual arts, social arts, some "elements" are isolated out of the flow of life and assembled more-or-less grammatically into objects and institutions to suit our purpose or our fancy.

This talk was given at a Festival of the International Cooperation Council in Pasadena in 1980.

Sometimes these human constructs become dysfunctional with the flow of life. The fenced-in land, for example, which is a human invention, shuts some people in and others out of natural resources, often turning people against each other in competition for survival. This construct of territory has taken on a malignant form, the militarized nation-state, causing an arms race that threatens to destroy a billion years of achievement for life on this planet.

Responding from the springs of life have come voices in the mountains calling for a new and different order in the world. New ideas trickle down and, fed by in-put from tributary sources, are turning into streams and rivers of a life force on its way to the ocean.

So where are we now? Having spent most of my life in what I consider the life-force movement for peace and justice in a new world order, I look around and see that we have actually come a long way since "peace" was a dirty word and "world government" a still, small voice in the mountains. Since 1945 the dysfunction of independent nations and irresponsible "free" enterprise in an interdependent world has become more and more obvious. The flow of movements to protect the environment and endangered species, including man, has increased. Peace, ecology and world government movements have gained support both among the masses and people in high places, and now I see these movements coming together tentatively in new coalitions and networks. This Festival is a visual example of coming together, and it may even be a catalytic event in transforming our diversity into a unity of purpose and common action. As I see it at present, however, this period of coalitions looks more like a marsh than a river, with more meandering networks of communication than concerted lines of action — a lowland of eddies and pools not going anywhere in particular. What we need is a channel that is deep and broad to give direction and momentum. And it must be strong enough to transform those malignant power structures of today into functional world institutions. Perhaps at this stage in our movement, that can be brought about intentionally with cooperation and a little luck.

Within the movement there are two distinguishable roads which, if they would converge, could create a mighty force; their goal to replace the independent, hostile systems of today with an organic world community which, like the ocean, would be a unity of diverse forms of life, an interdependent system harmonious with nature's flow. These roads I call the "High Road" and the "Low Road." The following observations are offered on some strengths and weaknesses of each, with suggestions of how and why they should converge.

The High Road aims directly at existing power structures to reach established "decision-makers" and through them to change the system. This road is straight and narrow and travelled mostly be well-informed and sophisticated people. Though small in number they are important because their analysis is usually clear and to the point, especially in distinguishing the basic cause from symptoms of dysfunction: the anomaly of independent nations running an interdependent world, as against the manifold evil results, like the arms race, rise of a military-industrial complex, secret agencies, corruption and violence. *By attacking the cause rather than merely protesting against the symptoms, these people are in a better position to effect a cure.* Furthermore, they have access to some centers of power in governments, in corporations and in the United Nations (which, though not itself a power, is a collecting place of independent powers). Travelling this road are organizations like Common Cause, New Directions and the World Federalists. They have had successes within countries (Watergate, Panama Canal Treaty, etc.) but very little success in relations between countries. Efforts since 1945 to change the U.N. Charter, for example, have shown few results, and there is no prospect for limiting the "sovereign right" of any nation in the U.N., even in President Carter's new project for U.N. "reform" which was instigated by the Federalists. The U.N. Special Session on Disarmament, which I attended throughout June, 1978, demonstrated the structural roadblock within the U.N. to disarmament: No official representative of a sovereign nation was willing — or able — to sacrifice one bullet of his country's independent security system for the larger good of the world community, or even for the good of his own people. There were simply not enough world citizens anywhere to make it politically feasible.

The Low Road, by contrast, is widespread and diverse. It meanders among the marshes, encompassing a variety of grass-roots

43

movements aiming at a new world order through the creation of new forms and institutions. Among these are the many New Age groups, human potential and liberation movements, spiritual and environmental communities, and world citizens generally. Reacting instinctively and emotionally to various facets of the anti-life force generated by the current anomaly, they tend to protest at the symptoms or withdraw from the power structure and experiment with new forms of living (vegetarianism, organic gardens, communes, etc.) Some are so disillusioned with government that they proclaim the right to "do your own thing" individually or in groups, embracing anarchy as the philosophy of the New Age. It is important to remember, however, that such freedom is not possible without the protection of government, and that does not now exist for ninety percent of the world's people. In fact, the pursuit of personal fulfillment is a luxury in the western world, bought at the expense of intolerable conditions elsewhere as democracy is suppressed and the basic necessities of life are not available. There is NO WAY to secure protection of individual freedoms without government, and there is NO WAY to manage the resources of an interdependent planet justly without world government. Retreat into anarchy, however idealistic, is sheer nostalgia and escapism in face of today's global problems. It is perhaps more responsible than anything else for the lack of momentum toward a new world order. Just as the High Road fails to relate to the people, the Low Road fails to relate to the actual or potential sources of power.

What is needed, as I see it, is for the High Road and the Low Road to "get it together" and go where the power is to change what is possible to change, and at the same time to start building new institutions from the ground up to insure that world government (that will come one way or another) shall not enforce uniformity, but provide a healthy balance of freedom and order, flow and form, compatible with nature and human potential. People must work together to make this happen. Powerful trends are against it, especially in the technology of death. Can people cross the artificial, man-made boundaries of nations, merging the strengths of High Road and Low, head and heart, analysis and instinct, strategy and numbers, into an effective force for life against death? The odds are long; the time

44

is short. But the life force is with us, and in the past it has won out.

What would it take now to make it happen? Some answers to this question are: **First, a common goal** that is basic, clear and communicable. So far this has not been articulated except, perhaps, in a negative form like avoiding common threats of nuclear or ecological catastrophes. Mobilization for Survival, for example, has listed "Zero Nuclear Weapons, Ban Nuclear Power, Stop the Arms Race, Fund Human Needs." These are surely targets to which most Low Roaders would agree, but are symptoms of a more basic problem which protest alone does not solve. The coalition of several world government organizations has come up with "The long-range goal we all share is lasting peace with justice through a democratic, federal world government to ensure complete, universal disarmament, human rights, environmental balance and economic equity." This is a positive statement that gets to the solution (world government) guaranteeing diversity within unity (federal) and human value (democratic). That says it all — for the High Road, at least.

Second, a cosmopolitan leadership is needed that spans the difference between High Road and Low, as well as differences within each. It is especially important that the leaders have a global perspective rather than a strictly national or parochial one. They are rare, but do exist already in people like Jacques Cousteau, Barbara Ward and Norman Cousins. There should be many more of them emerging out of the generation of "new consciousness."

Third, a broad popular enthusiasm is needed for universal values, transforming national patriotism into true humanism, with reverence for life and world citizenship added to other loyalties. This too could be emerging from the "new consciousness" and from the growing realization that problems of concern to different groups point to a common need for global solutions. In this context many of the Non-Governmental Organizations now accredited to the United Nations could play an important role. Trans-national in scope and larger in membership than most of the nations represented in the U.N. Assembly, they are a potential force for global commitment. (Some examples are: the International Cooperative Alliance with its 300 million members, the International Federation of Transport Workers with its 160 million, the Federation of Teachers with 5 million members.)

Fourth, disappearance of internecine rivalry among those who follow different paths to the same goal. Can we do what we ask nations to do, namely to subordinate special interests to the common purpose, at least to the point that we do not block each other's way? The tendency to disparage or patronize should give way to a feeling of teamwork among people who are engaged in different aspects of a very large project.*

Finally, it helps to have some good models of the community we are trying to build. The study and design of utopias is a valuable exercise. There has been increased interest in utopian experiments and literature in the 70's, and this is a good sign, like the light at the end of a long tunnel. In this connection I highly recommend A Constitution for the Federation of Earth. It is the most comprehensive plan I know and represents the work of an international body of citizens over ten years time, including many women as well as men. It was adopted and signed by 160 world citizens from 25 countries at Innsbruck, Austria in June, 1977, and is now being promoted as a basis for action.

How can we get all this together and on a road that's *going someplace?* We have here a great opportunity. The theme, "From Essence to Action"** suggests that the time has come. I think we can make it happen — for example, by determining:

1) to build deeper channels between the New Age groups that proclaim a wholistic or global perspective (world citizens by any other name) and all those political action groups working for a democratic, federal world government. It is especially important, I think, for the spiritually aware to become politically astute, so that politics is not confined to flat, two-dimensional issues but reflects the full height and depth of human potential.

2) to develop a sense of teamwork among those individuals

---

* A case in point is the World Government Organization Coalition which, since 1977, has engaged in cooperative planning and teamwork among some two dozen groups, here-to-fore at variance.
** *Theme of the Festival at which this talk was given.*

and groups that are working at different aspects of building the world community, whether they be saving the whales, expanding consumer cooperatives, or educating for global perspectives. The synergy process encourages this sense of teamwork, as does the town-meeting format of our World Citizen Assemblies that have met since 1975. Events like these should be planned so that they are cumulative in effect, gaining morale and momentum from each other.

3) to focus collective energy on a few key issues that are critical to survival and human potential, such as peace which requires world law, environmental health, human rights both political and economic, and the creation of world institutions to represent the interests of the people of the world across national boundaries. (An embryo People's Assembly was started across from the United Nations Assembly during the Special Session on Disarmament last summer, and others are already conceived or in labor.)

4) at the very least, we can determine to keep channels of communication open and clear of the sludge of petty, inter-organization rivalries!

In conclusion we could all say, "Let it begin with me, but not end with me." A drop of water is a fragile thing, but a river is irresistible on its way to the ocean. We cannot return to the Garden of Eden, but we can make it to the Ocean — a liveable world without unnecessary borders. After all, the Earth as seen from space by our own astronauts is "a beautiful blue planet." It is not a patchwork of pink, orange and purple blotches surrounded by dotted lines. It is, in fact, a unique "water planet" in which life like ours has taken four billion years to evolve. We, as stewards of this precious heritage, must secure it for the future by finding the way to live in harmony with nature and each other in a democratic world community.

Logo of the Global Community Center, Los Angeles

48

PART III

TO ABOLISH WAR

Look, if you give them a nuclear freeze, the next thing you know they'll want to outlaw war altogether.

TO OUTLAW WAR ALTOGETHER
THE LEGAL PRECEDENTS

Like many others, I watched with dismay what seemed like a run-away war machine in the early '80's with the Military Industrial Complex at the helm. Partial measures such as a nuclear freeze, arms "control" and disarmament appeared increasingly inadequate, even irrelevant. At this time I investigated the legal basis for outlawing war altogether through contacts made as a delegate to the Provisional World Parliament in Brighton, England in 1982. From their work I compiled a list of international precedents for outlawing war. This represents a turning point in my thinking.

"Look, if you give them a nuclear freeze, the next thing you know they'll want to outlaw war altogether." So goes the caption of a recent cartoon by Joseph Farris published in the *San Francisco Chronicle*. And that is exactly what some of them are trying to do. As a matter of fact, the legal basis already exists, and has existed for over a hundred years, for prohibiting weapons of mass destruction such as the nuclear, biological and chemical devices of modern warfare. The very same governments that are now manufacturing, stockpiling and threatening to use them have, by their own covenants, treaties and international laws, declared them illegitimate. If leaders of governments were tried today by the same principles that were used to try and execute war criminals after World War II, most of the leaders would be convicted as outlaws by the world community. The reason they have not been prosecuted is that the only courts available (including the so-called "World Court" in The Hague) are either national or international courts subordinated to the principle of national "sovereignty" which, like the "divine right of kings," puts governments above their own laws. Some enterprising lawyers and world citizens are attempting to change this.

As a first step in this process, some lawyers have compiled in legal form the international laws by which governments have limited their "right" to make war. A good example is *THE ILLEGALITY OF WAR* by William Durland (National Center on Law and Pacifism).[1] An-

---

* First presented as a keynote speech in Ottawa to the World Federalists of Canada, this was later printed in **Open Exchange**, a magazine serving the San Francisco Bay Area, Oct.-Dec. 1983, and in **Worldview Perspective**, spring of 1984.

1. National Center on Law and Pacifism. This book can be otained from the Association of World Citizens in San Francisco for $3.00 including postage. Write to 110 Sutter St., Suite 708, San Francisco, CA 94104.

other is the legal brief prepared by Leon Vickman, which will be referred to later. Both of these present the already-existing laws in a way that can be understood by the public. A summary of some of the laws cited is in the enclosed box at the end of this article.

These laws have been written and approved by governments. Some of them, like the Nuremberg Principles, have been applied and are still being applied with the force of law, as in the trials of former Nazis. They are not applied equally to victors as well as vanquished, even though those victors may be guilty of equal "crimes" such as the bombing of Hiroshima and Nagasaki and the installation of more awful weapons of mass destruction by the U.S., the U.S.S.R., and many others. This uneven application of international law is due to the lack of a true world court, as distinguished from national or international courts (The Hague).

Just and impartial application of the law requires:

(a) equal application of the principles to all parties under the law, and cannot operate merely by consent of the accused, as in the present International Court of Justice in The Hague;

(b) third party jurisdiction by impartial judges, which cannot be expected in national courtswhen the delinquent is the nation itself or its leaders.

While an initial requirement - that of a generally-accepted, known or written law - does already exist as outlined hereafter, these two other conditions do not. To remedy this latter situation takes a further step by lawyers and world citizens: namely, the development of extra-national courts which do not depend on the approval of nations, but act independently in the name of the people of the world community.

The widely publicized Bertrand Russell trials during the Vietnam War were an initiative in the evolution of extra-national tribunals, lifting the conscience of the world community without claiming any specific constituency or enforcement power. It was an educational and symbolic precedent for the development of extra-national courts. More structured in nature is the current action by Leon Vickman to establish a Provisional District World Court in Los Angeles under the mandate of a Provisional World Parliament which met in Brighton, England in 1982, representing a constituency of four million people across national boundaries. This Parliament was convened under a written *CONSTITUTION FOR THE FEDERATION OF EARTH* adopted by a cross-national body of people in 1977. On June 27 of 1983, the court issued summons to twenty-eight national governments which either possessed or were allegedly preparing to deploy nuclear weapons. The defendants named included all the major nuclear powers, such as the U.S., the U.S.S.R., the United Kingdom, France, and the Peoples Republic of China. The plaintiffs in this class action suit were listed as "The People of Earth." The chief counsel for the plaintiffs was California attorney, Leon L. Vickman, who filed the complaint on the basis of extensive documentation on the illegality of nuclear weapons under "commonly accepted international law together with newly emerging world law," some of which are listed in the enclosed box. Under the Summons, the defendant nations were given sixty days in which to reply, and a trial by jury was being set for sometime before the end of 1984. According to the rules of the Court, which are the same as for the U.S. Supreme Court, "Judgment by default will be taken against any defendant who may fail to file a responsive pleading as required by the Summons within the specified time."[2]

"Far from being an isolated action," Vickman stated, "the suit which we have entered is only the first of many which may be taken before Provisional District World Courts to defend the rights of humanity." Although the Nuremberg Tribunal which tried "war criminals" after World War II, and Bertrand Russell's Stockholm War Crimes Tribunal of the Vietnam War both give some important precedents for the present suit, these earlier actions were entirely ad hoc. The Provisional District World Courts are organized in the context of a constitution for world federation and an evolving world parliament, all of which is being implemented by stages . . . "to solve world problems peacefully and to serve the needs of humanity." Similar District World Courts are being projected by lawyers in Canada, India and Sri Lanka.[3]

Long before the first Provisional World Parliament met in 1982,

2. Leon L. Vickman, A Law Corporation, 16255 Ventura Blvd., Suite 605, Encino, CA 91436.

3. For further information, contact the World Constitution and Parliament Association, c/o Philip Isely, 1480 Hoyt Street, Suite 31, Lakewood, CO 80215.

the precedent for extra-national courts was established. This fact is documented in some detail in *THE COURT OF MAN*, published in 1973 by the Court of Man Foundation in Beverly Hills, California.[4] In it the author, Gerald H. Gottlieb says, "History shows that many courts, from earliest times to the recent past, were direct and extra-national courts of the community itself. Unlike the modern national and international courts, those extra-national courts of history did not require the consent or permission of States in order to exist and adjudicate. Indeed, it happens that man's past is full of examples of courts operating independently, arising earlier than or separate from formal governments, and taking jurisdiction wider than the territories of States." He cites, for example, the Indo-Europeans who invaded India, the Hebrews, the early Romans, Greeks, Celts, Germans, Frisians, Swedes, Danes, Norwegians, Icelanders, Anglo-Saxons, and various African tribes. These extra-national courts were created to respond to the needs of the times. Gottlieb says, "A seeming urgency among people can bring them at critical moments to form or support tribunals even before creating governments or becoming subordinate to kings; in part they are motivated by the need to have disputes settled so that the routines of social and economic life, their daily pursuits, may be resumed." The need for law is compelling and now exists on a world basis. Advanced by technology, communications, commerce, and promoted by numerous non-governmental institutions which are already global in their concerns, the need for law is made especially urgent by the increased awareness of common dangers from aggression and from wrongs against humanity. "The more foreboding these dangers," Gottlieb says, "the more immediate becomes the felt necessity for law's practical judgments."

In face of the threat to all life on this planet from the arsenals of mass destruction, there is an immediate necessity to assert the accountability of nations and their leaders to the world community. This is being done, first, by publicizing the already-existing international laws that outlaw weapons of mass destruction and war itself and, second, by creating extra-national courts that will apply these laws to nations in the name of the people of the world. World courts acting for the world community could provide a means of settling international disputes without resorting to war, by making it incumbent on

---

4. Court of Man Foundation, Inc., 9595 Wilshire Blvd., Beverly Hills, CA 90210

nations to obey the laws they themselves have made.

Law itself is not the maximum standard of what is right and good –that is the province of philosophy, religion, and the arts. Law is the *minimum essential* for survival of the community, for it is the civilized way of resolving conflicts. Without it any dispute can escalate into violence and war. The prospect of that happening today is a global holocaust virtually ending the experiment of life on this planet.

The time has come TO OUTLAW WAR ALTOGETHER.

Legal Precedents

The Declaration of St. Petersberg, 1868, declared that "the only legitimate object ... (of) war is to weaken the military forces of the enemy;" indicating that weapons of indiscriminate destruction are "contrary to the laws of humanity."

The Hague Convention, 1899 & 1907, binding for all major powers, expressly forbids nations: (a) To employ poison or poisoned weapons, (b) To kill or wound treacherously ... (c) To employ arms projectiles or material calculated to cause unnecessary suffering..."

The Treaty of Peace with Germany 1917 & 1925 Protocol condemns "the use in war of poisonous gases, and all analagous liquids, materials or devices" and strictly forbids their manufacture and importation in Germany.

The Kellogg-Briand Pact, 1928, signed by the U.S. and 42 other countries, "condemns recourse to war for the solution of international controversies, and renounces it as an instrument of national policy."

The Nuremberg Principles, 1945, applied in the trials of German "war criminals" and introduced by the U.S. delegation to the United Nations General Assembly in 1946, where it was unanimously adopted; outlines violations of international law for which even individual citizens of belligerent nations could be held responsible. These include (a) Crimes Against Peace: namely, planning, preparation ... of a war of aggression; (b) War Crimes: namely, violations of the laws and customs of war, such as ill-treatment of civilian populations and wanton destruction of cities; and (c) Crimes Against Humanity: namely, murder, extermination ... and other inhuman acts committed against any civilian population before or during the war ... whether or not in violation of the domestic law of the country where perpetrated.

The United Nations Charter, 1945, adopted "to ensure ... that armed force shall not be used, save in the common interest" (Preamble), and in Article 2 "the members agree to ... refrain in their international relations from the threat or use of force..."

The McCloy-Zorin Agreed Principles, 1961, presented to the U.N. General Assembly by the U.S. and U.S.S.R. and adopted unanimously, calls for "general and complete disarmament" accompanied by "effective arrangements for the maintenance of peace in accordance with the principles of the Charter of the United Nations."

Article 9 of The Japanese Constitution, 1947, "forever renounce(s) war as a sovereign right of a nation and the threat or use of force as means of settling international disputes." It states unequivocally, "The right of belligerency of the state will not be recognized." While this is the most radical statement of the limitation of national sovereignty (except by the Provisional World Parliament), there are such statements in the constitutions of other countries, for example: India (Article 51), Costa Rica (12), Belgium (25), France (55 and Preamble), Italy (11), Luxemberg, (7), Norway (93), Germany (24).

The Provisional World Parliament Bill Number One, 1982, "To outlaw nuclear weapons and other weapons of mass destruction" passed unanimously by delegates representing 4 million people without regard to national boundaries. According to a legal brief, "This landmark legislation merely declared what was already 'world law'."

EMPOWERING PEACE

Appalled by the surrealism of the arms race and the incredible contradiction between a public consensus that nuclear war is not survivable and acquiescence in the biggest military build-up in history; moved, too, by the impact of films being released to mass audiences such as "The Last Epidemic, "Testament," "Threads," "The Day After," I look to some insights from Greek tragic drama and myth in groping for a way out of this global nightmare.

As we celebrate the convening of the United Nations in 1945 "to save succeeding generations from the scourge of war," what can we say about "empowering peace"? The Preamble to the UN Charter declares that "armed force shall not be used save in the common interest," and Article 2 adds, "All members shall refrain in their international relations from the threat or use of force..."

Yet, in the last 40 years the world has gone literally mad. How mad is brought to mind by a recent article in the *San Francisco Chronicle*, "Air Force's Proposal for a Huge Buried Base"–$50 billion for the ability to retaliate AFTER a nuclear war has been fought. Next to this article is a column headed, "1 of 5 Adults in U.S. Suffers Mental Problem." And no wonder! I ask you, which is crazier, the ones who would have the last word in a nuclear war, or the one in five who can't cope in this mad, mad world?

According to a survey by the Public Agenda Foundation, a nonpartisan research organization, and the Center for Foreign Policy Development at Brown University, the American Public is "clear and resolute" in believing, at a "consensus level" (96 to 3) that "picking a fight with the Soviet Union is too dangerous in a nuclear world" and that if the U.S. "had a bigger nuclear arsenal than the Soviets, they

A talk given on United Nations Sunday, October 21, 1984 at the 1st Unitarian Church of Berkeley, California would simply keep building until they caught up." As columnist Tom Wicker asks, "Why should an American public that considers nuclear war 'unwinnable, horrible, unsurvivable' apparently be preparing to re-elect a president ... who has presided over the most expensive American military buildup in history?" This is hardly an example of "empowering peace." How then can we get back into focus the determination "to save succeeding generations from the scourge of war"?

The only way to empower peace, I am convinced, is to ABOLISH WAR ITSELF–IN OUR TIME–BY THE YEAR 2000. All half-way measures like the "freeze" and arms control must be put into this perspective, for none of them can of themselves prevent a catastrophe. I think it can be done in this century, just as slavery was abolished in the last century against many of the vested interests and arguments about "human nature" and "unchangeable" institutions. As cannibalism and other evils have been abolished forever by generations past, our generation is charged inescapably with the abolition of war. For another generation, it will be too late.

We KNOW now: the implications of "The Last Epidemic."*

We KNOW that we are reaching a condition of irreversible damage to the environment. It has been amply documented in the Global 2000 Report.

We KNOW that we can reach a point of no return at any time in the East-West paranoia, and likewise in the North-South confrontation between rich and poor, between the well-fed and the starved.

We KNOW all this. We have NO excuse. It may be said of us one day, "Forgive them not, for they KNOW what they do."

The current struggle of the peace movement may be the most important of all time. It is like the climax to a Greek drama, that scene from Aeschylus' play where Athena transformed the Furies, those demons of tribal vengeance, into the "Eumenides" or "well-tempered ones," origin of a jury system of law and justice. We, the Chorus, will have the final word for, as in Greek drama it is the people, not the actors, that determine the meaning of the play.

Governments will not abolish war, for they are its instruments, caught up like the Furies in their own fate. The United Nations itself, alas, has become a stage for this fateful game we call "Chicken." Only the voice of the people, inherently without nation or race, speaking in accents loud and clear can change the name and nature of the game, as it has done before.

The voice that speaks for the future is the voice of the Promethean element in human nature. According to Greek mythology, Prometheus gave to humans the one distinctive quality by which they could surpass the animals and survive; that quality is foresight, or imagination–the ability to look to the future, the ability to ask, not "Are you better off now?" but "Will your children be better off tomorrow?" and "Will your grandchildren be better off The Day After?"*

Everyone on this earth is born a citizen of the world. Those who recognize their responsibility to it might be called "born-again world citizens," and they are growing everywhere in numbers and in consciousness. The time has come when "We the People" must re-assert our determination "to save succeeding generations from the scourge of war." Nothing less than the ABOLITION OF WAR IN OUR TIME can possibly fulfill our obligation as trustees of life on this planet.

---

* *These titles refer to current films on the effects of nuclear war.*

Logo of the International Cooperation Council to 1979

FROM ARMED TRUCE TO PERMANENT PEACE

In a panel discussion at the Academy of World Studies, San Francisco, I tried to marshall "rational" arguments for the total abolition of war: the cost of buying time, treating causes instead of symptoms, cost effectiveness. The U.S. transition from confederacy to federation and the impending European federation are cited, along with quotations from world leaders, to make the case.

Since the end of World War II, this planet has survived in a state of armed truce. Most of the efforts for peace in the last forty years have not been designed to change this situation, only to prolong it. Consider, for example, "deterrence," arms "control," nuclear "freeze." Even the United Nations, which was supposed to "maintain international peace and security" (Article I), has presided over an extended balance of terror because it was not given the power to maintain permanent peace.

Buying Time But At What Price?

At best these programs are buying time, and that is important. But, it should be asked, at what price? Eight hundred billion dollars a year worldwide for arms, a two trillion dollar deficit in the USA alone, unmet human needs, unsolved ecological crises, and a mortgage that will take future generations centuries to repay–these are the cost of the time we are buying. I submit that we had better look hard at what we do with the time so dearly purchased.

---

* This talk was given at the Academy of World Studies, San Francisco, and published in the Academy's magazine, *Worldview Perspective*, fall of 1985.

This time is too precious to be spent merely in protesting. The horror of modern war and danger of the arms race are known already. As far back as the nineteen-fifties a cartoon pictured "Humanity" nailed to a cross marked "Nuclear War" with the caption, "Forgive them NOT - for they know what they do!" We must do more than object to what is unacceptable.

We Must Go Beyond Partial Measures That Ameliorate Rather Than Eliminate War

We must also go beyond the partial measures that are aimed at ameliorating war rather than eliminating it. A nuclear freeze, for example, even if successful would leave a stockpile of weapons in the US and USSR equivalent to one and a half million Hiroshima-size bombs ready to go off. And arms "control" simply means controlled increase in that stockpile of weapons. Nuclear disarmament would leave biological and chemical weapons that could wipe out much of the human race. Even general and complete disarmament would leave the technological possibility of rearmament. The arms race by itself, though its weapons were never used, could precipitate human and ecological disasters as terminal as war.

Furthermore, we must go beyond treating the symptoms instead of the causes of war - symptoms such as refugees and other victims, hunger, street crime, militarism. We cannot ignore the human tragedies and aberrations that are the conditions of armed truce, but we must go beyond them. It is not enough to bind up the wounds - to put bandaids on the cancer. We must get to the cause of war and its cure, even if it requires surgery.

Time To Focus On The Abolition of War Itself

The time has come to focus on the abolition of war itself. Just as the institution of slavery was abolished decisively in the last century, and cannibalism, infanticide and other evils before it, so the institution of war (surely the worst of all human inventions) must now be abolished unequivocally, completely, before it abolishes the human race.

We must get to the root of the problem. That root, I believe,

62

is not human nature, or a matter of "good guys vs bad guys" or "us vs. them." It is a matter of structure. This ecosystem we call Earth, made more and more interdependent by modern technology (especially of weapons), has outgrown the system of independent sovereign nations which still persists, causing a malevolent, cancerous arms race. The system is no longer functional. The affairs of an interdependent world cannot possibly be managed by one hundred-sixty independent and competing states, even through their well-intentioned surrogate, the United Nations. The system itself is obsolete!

Anarchy Produces War–The Alternative Is Law

Each sovereign nation acting as a law-unto-itself produces anarchy. Anarchy with nuclear (or other) weapons produces war. War with nuclear (or biological or chemical) weapons means the END of billions of years of evolution on this planet–of everything we hold dear.

The alternative to war is and has always been LAW, the civilized method of settling disputes. It involves some generally accepted principles, third party jurisdiction by impartial judges, and a system of courts with power to enforce their judgments on individual violators without, as in war, wreaking vengeance on whole populations. It requires a minimum sacrifice of the independent "right" to make war and an obligation to live within the limits of the laws agreed upon. Its reward is peace and collective survival.

Hundreds of Precedents Show That It Works

And it works! There are hundreds of precedents that show how it works. A city like San Francisco does not go to war against Los Angeles over water rights. There are peaceful alternatives for settling their dispute such as laws, courts and ballots. Furthermore, California does not arm itself against Arizona, New Mexico, Colorado, Nevada, and Utah, although these are states which contain nuclear weapons. Yet they all live in fear of countries on the other side of the world and arm together against them. The reason is that the civilized alternatives are not in effect at present for resolving disputes among the *nations*. Conflicts of interest will always exist among nations, as they do among cities and states, but they need not lead to war. President Harry Truman said in 1945: "It will be just as easy for nations to get along in a Republic of the World as it is for you to get along in the Republic of the United States." He thus expressed a hope that existed at the founding of the United Nations, which is still to be realized.

There Are Already Precedents In International Law

As a matter of fact, some of the requirements for a rule of law among nations do already exist. Weapons of mass destruction have been declared "contrary to the laws of humanity" by the Declaration of St. Petersberg in 1869 and by the Hague Conventions of 1899 and 1907. The latter would bind all major nuclear powers. War itself has been "outlawed" by nations in the Kellogg-Briand Pact of 1928, the Nuremberg Principles, and the United Nations Charter of 1945. And "general and complete disarmament" under "effective arrangements for the maintenance of peace" was agreed to by all members of the United Nations in 1961 when they approved the US/USSR sponsored McCloy-Zorin Principles. [For further information on these and other laws against war, see *THE ILLEGALITY OF WAR* by William Durland and other sources listed in a previous article, *To Outlaw War Altogether*. These are available from the Association of World Citizens, 110 Sutter Street, Suite 708, San Francisco, CA 94104.]

An international Court of Justice already exists in The Hague, and there is a Human Rights Court in Europe to which national governments can be taken for violation of accepted international laws. What does not yet exist is the power to enforce the decisions of these courts against recalcitrant leaders of the sovereign nations. While Europe is moving rapidly from a community of sovereign states to a federal "United States of Europe," the United Nations remains a confederacy "based on the principle of sovereign equality of all its members" (Article 2:1) and therefore unable to enforce decisions of the International Court, its own creation.

There Are Also Precedents For Transformation From Confederacy To Federal Government

There are precedents for the transformation of a confederacy into a federal government. The United States celebrates the two-hundredth anniversary of such a transformation in 1987. The founding fathers had the wisdom to make the change from a system that didn't work (for the same reason the United Nations doesn't work) into a federal government that does work. Australia is another example, where the transition was made about 1900 due, in part, to the problems of building a trans-continental railway. Under the confederacy the states determined the width of the tracks, and trains had to change at each border. It took a federal government to make the trains run on a common gauge - to make the country "work." The experience of Europe is also worth noting. Having been the battleground of nations for centuries and the scene of two world wars, it has been without a single war since creation of the Council of Europe in 1949. While it is not yet a federal system, its heads of state met in 1985 to strengthen the present European Community along federalist lines by coordinating foreign and defense policies, abolishing the requirement for unanimity in decisions, and increasing the power of the democratically elected Parliament of Europe. War is almost as unthinkable today between France and Germany as it is between California and Nevada.

Realism Is Measured By Cost Effectiveness. The Current War System Is Not Realistic By This Standard

We are living on borrowed time. The best way to spend it, I think, is to build the alternatives to war–the systems for resolving conflicts by civilized means, namely: laws, courts, ballots and democratic, federal government. The usual reaction to such a proposition is that it seems like a good idea but is simply "unrealistic," at least in the foreseeable future (meaning fifty to five hundred years).

Most Americans take pride in being realistic. And "realistic" is measured by cost-effectiveness. What of an enterprise that costs three hundred billion dollars a year, creates a two trillion dollar deficit, produces less rather than more of the security it is supposed to increase, creates products which, if not used in ten to fifteen years become obsolete, and if used would destroy the users along with the targets? Cost-effective? Who in his right mind would buy stock in such an enterprise? A top financial advisor to the US government has been quoted as saying (on his retirement) that if the government were judged as a business enterprise, most of the top executives would be in jail!

For the alternative to war to be successful, it would require investment in planning, in vigilance, in trust and in some initial sacrifice of national sovereignty–surely not too high a price to pay for a better, even very good chance for survival of life on earth.

Some Prominent Leaders Have Recognized The Needs For Enforceable World Law

According to Arthur Schopenhauer, all truth passes through three stages:
1. It is ridiculed.
2. It is violently opposed.
3. It is accepted as being self-evident.

Fortunately, the need to abolish war by creating the necessary conditions of permanent peace –enforceable world law and world government– has become self-evident to some people in positions of authority:

Secretary-General of the United Nations, U Thant said: "World Federalists hold before us the beacon of a unified mankind living in peace under a just world order....The heart of their program–a world under law–is realistic and attainable."

President Dwight D. Eisenhower said: "The world no longer has a choice between force and law; if civilization is to survive, it must choose the rule of law."

Winston Churchill said: "Unless some effective supranational government can be set up and brought quickly into action, the prospects for peace and human progress are dark and doubtful."

Mikhail Gorbachev, at a 1985 rally of Soviet war veterans, declared: "A world without wars and weapons is attainable in practice ....Detente is needed, but only as a transitional stage from a world cluttered with arms to a reliable and all-embracing system of international security."

And finally, *General Douglas MacArthur:* "Many will tell you with mockery and ridicule that the abolition of war can only be a dream ... that it is the vague imagination of a visionary, but we must go on or we will go under. We must have new thoughts, new ideas, new concepts. We must have sufficient imagination and courage to translate the universal wish for peace–which is rapidly becoming a universal necessity–into actuality."

Registration Card, International Registry of World Citizens, Paris

THE NEW ABOLITIONISTS
SOME LESSONS FROM THE 19TH CENTURY

This was a more ambitious research project, occasioned by my turn to give a paper at the venerable Berkeley Outlook Club (of which I was the first woman member and, in 1989, first woman president). It forced me to reflect over my (then) fifty years in the peace movement and possible parallels to the anti-slavery movement. The slow build-up, the factions, the vested interests, the obstacles, the personalities, the role of religious groups — all provided insight and perspective. The lessons? No one was in control — ever, but somehow it came out right!

"All truth passes through three stages," according to Arthur Schopenhauer: "First, it is ridiculed. Second, it is violently opposed. Third, it is accepted as being self-evident."

Today it seems self-evident that slavery is unacceptable as a social institution. Yet little more than a century ago it was an issue that tore this country apart in a civil war. And a century before that it was an opinion held by a very few "eccentric" individuals, mostly Quakers. Similarly, other social institutions such as cannibalism, human sacrifice and child labor have become absolutely unacceptable in most societies. It is the thesis of this paper that war, the greatest evil of all time, is becoming absolutely unacceptable, and that lessons can be learned from the Abolitionist Movement of the 19th century about how this may come about.

After fifty years of personal involvement in the peace movement, I have come to the conclusion that nothing short of the abolition of war itself can possibly fulfill this generation's obligation to the future. This conclusion was reinforced by adoption of "Abolition of War" as their focus by the World Citizens Assembly and the World

---

* Paper given to the Outlook Club of Berkeley, California in April, 1985 and published in the 20th Anniversary Issue of *Worldview Perspective*, Academy of World Studies, San Francisco, 1988.

Federalists of the United States and Canada in their 1984 conventions, as well as by the positive response to an ensuing "new abolitionist" campaign. The reason for concentrating on complete abolition of war rather than other more limited steps in that direction is that the latter cannot protect against what is already an absolutely unacceptable risk to life on this planet. This should be self-evident from the fact that the arsenals, even if frozen at current levels could destroy that life many times over; that "arms control" simply means controlled increase in that capacity; that nuclear disarmament would leave absolutely unacceptable amounts of chemical, biological and other weapons intact; and that even if, by some unforeseeable miracle, the weapons above were never used, the mere accumulation of them is enough to destroy the resources needed now to forestall human and ecological catastrophes that would be as terminal as nuclear war. The evidence is overwhelming — and has been for years. It cannot be ignorance that has made the century so slow to face the necessity of abolishing war. It must be something psychological — individual and collective — that goes through a painfully long process to arrive at the acceptance of a "self evident" truth. Just as the cruelties of the slave trade were a matter of record long before they were admitted and acted upon, so it is with the abominations of war. For this reason I have chosen to look at the progress of the anti-slavery movement of the 19th century for whatever insight it can provide into the anti-war movement today.

The Past Provides a Perspective on the Present But History is Not a Cyclical Process

The past is no crystal ball for the future, but it does provide a perspective on the present, some parallels in relation to problems and obstacles, and some lessons from experiences of failure and success. It may also provide interesting and amusing anecdotes and incidents *deja vu*. For all these reasons I have taken the Abolitionist Movement of the 19th century as a kind of case study, understanding well that a more thorough history of this and other similar movements could revise some of my "insights."

Finally, I must admit my own assumption that history is not a cyclical process going nowhere, but a lineal process, however irregular, leading generally upward. I believe, in other words, that there is an evolving consciousness that has somehow moved from inert to living matter, from plants to animals, from water-based to land-based species and upward in intelligence to the human species. I see no reason why this process should stop with man (or woman) and, in fact, I believe that a rising moral and spiritual consciousness is recognizable through history, even accelerating in our time as evidenced by the movements for human and animal rights and protection of nature. Perhaps this reflects my own evolution more than my understanding of history, but even after fifty years in the peace movement I remain an unregenerate optimist over the long haul. Meanwhile, for the short haul, it seems that we barely muddle through.

From 1619 To the Nineteenth Century the Build-Up of Opposition to Slavery Was Slow–Even the Constitutional Convention Was Not Used

In looking back at the Abolish Slavery Movement, a brief chronology of events is instructive. The following is taken mostly from a book by Merton L. Dillon called, "The Abolitionists: The Growth of a Dissenting Minority" (W.W. Norton, N.Y. 1974).

In the first stage, from 1619 when the first Negro slave was imported to Virginia through the 18th century, there was a long, slow build-up of conscientious moral opposition by individuals, mostly Quakers. By 1750, Quakers in general were opposed to slavery and in 1775 they organized the first anti-slavery society in Philadelphia. According to Dillon the Quakers dominated the movement until well into the 19th century, insisting on a non-violent, educational approach with the intention of converting slave holders through rational and moral "friendly persuasion." In this Age of Reason and Enlightenment, the anti-slavery forces failed to use the Constitutional Convention of 1787, assuming that the founding fathers would do so. The Founding Fathers, however, were too anxious to avoid alienating the southerners, and Benjamin Franklin himself refused to introduce a resolution on the grounds that it would do "more harm than good by

71

exciting the suspicions of southern members." The final product even gave slaveholders 3/5 of a vote per slave, giving the holders control of Congress up to the Civil War.

The Anti-Slavery Movement Ran Into Opposition From Vested Interests In the Nineteenth Century

In the early 19th century, the movement ran into opposition from vested interests, "property rights" and racism. The growth of the cotton industry in the south and the mercantile trade in the north were both based on slave labor, and opposition to slavery was branded as "un-American." Young people were "more interested in wealth than principle" according to Dillon, and although emancipation laws were gradually introduced in the North and foreign slave trade was prohibited by Congress in 1807, the laws were poorly enforced, and "there were more failures than successes after 1800." (Dillon, Introduction, 3-30) Various gradualist approaches came into being, such as that of the American Colonization Society, founded in 1817 to settle free Negroes in Africa. These were later condemned as "racist" being based on adherence to the idea of Negro inferiority. The supporters of colonization were accused by James G. Birney of being half-hearted anti-slavery men "who would abolish slavery only in the abstract, and somewhere about the middle of the future." (from Birney's Letters, I, 202, quoted by Dillon, 63).

The Movement Came Into Focus in the 1830's

The movement really came into focus in the 1830's, beginning with the publication of *The Liberator* in 1831 by William Lloyd Garrison, an abrasive, uncompromising abolitionist who became a pivotal force, proclaiming through his paper slogans of immediate and unconditional emancipation. In his first editorial, Garrison flung out his strident challenge to the land:

"Let Southern oppressors tremble — let their secret abettors tremble — let their Northern apologists tremble ... I will be as harsh as truth, and as uncompromising as justice. On this subject, I do not wish to think, or speak, or write, with moderation. Tell a man whose wish to think, or speak, or write, with moderation. Tell a man whose house is on fire to give a moderate alarm ... I am in earnest. I will not equivocate — I will not excuse — I will not retreat an inch — AND I WILL BE HEARD."

This one man's voice aroused the nation as nothing before. People "were startled by this avenging angel, an inflexible figure from a Puritan mold. His language was furious, almost Biblical. He whipped and goaded the conscience of a people. He made them listen ....Garrison raised the struggle against slavery above politics and compromise. He admitted no shadings of right and wrong. Slavery was total evil and had to be obliterated immediately and forever....The founding of *The Liberator* was a knife stroke cutting all ties with the past. Now the nation had to face itself." (Lader, The Bold Brahmins, 46-47)

Confrontations were inevitable and often violent. The following quote from "a prominent New York businessman" shows why:

"We are not such fools as to know that slavery is a great evil, a great wrong. But it was consented to by the founders of our Republic. ....A great portion of the property of the Southerners is invested under its sanction; and the business of the North, as well as the South, has become adjusted to it. There are millions upon millions of dollars due from Southerners to the merchants and mechanics of this city alone, the payment of which would be jeopardized by any rupture between the North and the South. We cannot afford, sir, to let you and your associates succeed in your endeavour to overthrow slavery. It is not a matter of principle with us. It is a matter of business necessity....We mean, sir, to put you abolitionists down - by fair means if we can, by foul means if we must." (As quoted in Lader, 27)

Even the "liberal" press attacked Garrison:

"For the abolitionists 'ought not to defy the public, however wrong,' preached the Christian Register, a Unitarian paper. 'In what terms of indignation,' cried the Boston Evening Transcript, 'can we speak of the man, who, by rancorous denunciations, and his brawling, ferocious abuse, together with the disorganizing tendencies of his doctrines, has excited the people to such an ebullition of their deeply exasperated feelings.'" (Ibid, 28)

Opposition Served to Increase Support For the Abolitionists

Opposition served both to increase support for the Abolitionists and to diffuse the motives for doing so. No longer was it a simple matter of morality, but matters also of freedom of speech, states rights, interpretation of constitutional law and, increasingly, open hostility against the South. Just as mob reaction to Abolitionists revealed new anti-slavery sympathizers, so Southern resistance to anti-slavery efforts, both in and out of Congress, contributed to the growth of the movement. (Dillon, 100)

The Movement Became Politicized by 1840

By 1840, the movement was becoming politicized, and the Liberty Party was organized, nominating James G. Birney, a radical Abolitionist, for president. In a speech in defense of the Party in 1844, Arnold Buffam explained its purpose:

"The American Liberty Party is not (as it is often demonstrated by our opponents) a third party. We are the true original American Party, seeking to carry out the principles of our forefathers, as set forth in the Declaration of Independence. These principles have for a long time been lost sight of, in the fog of two great parties, which are working with each other for the mastery, not for the promotion of the cause of liberty but for the establishment of a domineering Oligarchy, and for the perpetuation of the old monarchical and aristocratic doctrine, that the well-born and the rich have a right to tyrannize over the poor, and to appropriate to themselves the product of their labor ..." (Quoted in Pease, 424)

The Party was not very successful. Numbering only 7,100 members in 1840, it reached its high-water mark of 65,000 votes in the election of 1843, and a year later won enough votes in New York (15,000) to defeat Clay and throw the election to Polk. (Thomas, 94) But when the Mexican War, which was dubbed "Mr. Polk's War" of 1846-48 broke out, the political Abolitionists conducted fervent but minority opposition to it as a "slaveholders' war" and became even more convinced "that no anti-slavery measures and no measures beneficial to the North could be anticipated from any political party which felt itself dependent on southern votes." (Hawkins, 162)

Other political methods were tried, such as petitions to Congress also with only moderate success due to a "Gag Rule," imposed by the majority, tabling all anti-slavery petitions. John Quincy Adams, known as "Mad Man of Massachusetts," conducted a one-man campaign in the House of Representatives for eight years, until the Gag Rule was finally rescinded in 1844 by a vote of 105-80. (Lader, Chapter VII) While the petitions languished, Adams, by his spectacular battle had opened the halls of Congress to the slavery debate, taken it from the moral arena of Garrison and forced it into the fulcrum of national politics. Shrewd realism, however, kept Adams from complete alignment with the Abolitionists. As early as 1839, he had submitted three radical resolutions to the House, setting July 4, 1842 as the date after which any child born to slave parents would be declared free, prohibiting future slave states (except Florida) and declaring slavery illegal in the District of Columbia after July 4, 1845. According to Lader, "It was an eminently practical plan of gradual abolition, but the House ignored it. With it probably disappeared one of the last comprehensive chances for a peaceful settlement of the crisis." (Lader, 99)

The End of the 1840's Brought Increasing Support for a Slave Uprising

By the end of the 1840's, Abolitionists were losing faith in moral persuasion, non-resistance, even political action. There was growing support for a slave uprising. "Is it wrong to resist oppression unto blood?," Garrison asked in 1837. "A voice from Bunker Hill cries No! The gory soil of Lexington and Concord thunders No!" (Dillon, 223) John Brown's raid at Harper's Ferry in 1859 contributed to the crisis atmosphere. It confirmed the fear that southerners had of direct anti-slavery aggression. At the same time, the specter that had haunted them since 1820 had attained reality; the Republicans would carry the presidential election; the only recourse for southern radicals was secession. "Brown's raid played into the hands of those radicals who insisted on the South's leaving the Union. They were not deterred from their plans by the fact that most Republican leaders repudiated Brown and disclaimed abolitionism.

The Republican Convention of 1860 wrote into the Party platform a plank denouncing the Harper Ferry raid, and Abraham Lincoln even accepted Brown's execution as being just, 'even though he agreed ... in thinking slavery wrong.'" (Dillon, 242) But the Civil War broke out in 1861, and on September 22, 1862, following the Union victory at the Battle of Antietam, Lincoln issued a preliminary Emancipation Proclamation "as a fit and necessary war measure," declaring all slaves in areas still in rebellion on January 1, 1863, "then, henceforth, and forever free." His motives were mixed. In part, they were military aimed at dividing the Confederacy and depriving them of black manpower. In part, they were political aimed at persuading European liberals and radical republicans that the war was being fought to end slavery. But the proclamation also evidenced Lincoln's own advancing awareness of anti-slavery sentiment. For this the abolitionists could take much credit according to Dillon. (256)

Emancipation, far from being the result of a morally transformed America, as its early proponents had intended, served instead to justify many prevailing values and perpetuate the ruling order. The Reconstruction effort to transform southern political and social affairs was gradually abandoned and the southern states were allowed to resume management of their race relations so that the status of the freedmen rapidly deteriorated. Observing this development, Frederick Douglass, for one, was not surprised. "Liberty came to the freedmen of the United States, not in mercy but in wrath," he exclaimed, "not by moral choice but by military necessity....Nothing was to have been expected other than what has happened." (Dillon 264) And yet, "Despite these ambiguities," Dillon concludes, "the anti-slavery movement's reputed success in destroying an ancient, entrenched institution provided inspiration for later nineteenth century reformers who sought to eradicate other evils." (Ibid, 265) The evil of slavery, at least, had been overcome and a new level of awareness, imperfect though it was, had been established in human society.

What Insights Can be Derived From This Short History?

First of all, I found that what started with a clear moral imperative in the consciences of a few individuals, became complicated by a wide variety of motives as the movement expanded. Some of the motives were quite compatible, if not identical, with the revulsion against slavery, such as reaction against suppression of free speech and against violence perpetrated on abolitionists. Others were not so closely related, such as power struggles within and between organizations, including churches, women's groups and political factions. Others were even antithetical to the original moral intentions, such as hatred of the southern aristocracy and advocacy of violent uprising by the slaves. Even the final Emancipation Proclamation could be attributed more to military than to moral motives.

Second, it is noteworthy that as the movement gained momentum it became more and more impossible to control. The American Anti-Slavery Society, founded by William Lloyd Garrison in 1833 on the doctrine of "no union with slaveholders," was split in 1840 by the American and Foreign Anti-Slavery Society led by James G. Birney, who directed its energies through the churches and the Union. Other divisions followed: The Free Soil Party, or Political Abolitionists, and the Liberty Party, or Gerrit Smith School of Abolitionists ... and on and on. The variety of anti-slavery sects was outlined in a lecture by Frederick Douglass to the Rochester Ladies' Anti-Slavery Society. (Thomas, 126-131) As the issue followed the opening of new territories to the West and South with local contests over whether they would be slave or free, the movement itself became increasingly out of control by any one individual or group — perhaps an indication of the vitality as well as diversity of the movement.

On the other hand, the movement seemed to gain momentum as the issue itself became more focused on total abolition. Partial and reform-type measures like those of the Society for the Relief of Free Negroes Unlawfully Held in Bondage, and the moderate, church-oriented (Congregational) American Union for Relief and Improvement of the Colored Race, and the American Colonization Society did not arouse much enthusiasm. Nor did efforts to humanize the treatment of slaves or appeal to their owners' reason and conscience, or to provide better education for Negroes both in the North and the South. It was Garrison's trumpet call for complete abolition and "no union with slaveholders" that lit the fire, and *The Liberator* became the center of a firestorm.

Personalities Had a Major Role in the Movement

Personalities, I found, had a lot to do with the strength of the movement. Garrison did much to fan it into flames by his relentless rhetoric. He exhibited an almost joyful sense of destiny. He was described by an early rival as "Lloyd Garrulous ... a great egotist," displaying "the pert loquacity of a bluejay." He wrote of himself "...my name shall one day be known to the world....This, I know, will be deemed excessive vanity - but time shall prove it prophetic." He was not reckless, but he could face martyrdom almost joyfully, opening one letter, for example, "My dear partner in the joys and honors of persecution." (Lader 17-18) Garrison was undoubtedly the most effective single person in bringing the movement into focus. From his time on there was no question that the goal was abolition. The factional contests were on matters of strategy.

Another effective personality was John Quincy Adams who waged battle single handedly in the House of Representatives until the Gag order was rescinded in 1844. He was described as old before his time, short, paunchy and almost bald, his voice always shrill and his temper increasingly short — "Fierce as ten furies, terrible as hell," Andrew Jackson put it. And Adams himself admitted in his diary, "I have need of perpetual control over passion." (Lader, 87) "His epithets lashed the House unmercifully. One Representative, a leading proponent of the Gag, was attacked by Adams for 'emitting a half hour of his rotten breath.' Another was branded, 'the very thickest skull of all New Hampshire.' A third, cried Adams, kept 'butting his head against the air like a he-goat.'" (Ibid, 91) Eight years he fought, but in the end he won not only the end of the Gag Rule, but the opening of Congress to the whole slavery debate.

Also worthy of mention are two women, Sarah and Angelina Grimke, for their effectiveness in advancing the cause–not only of Abolition but also of women's liberation. These two fragile sisters from South Carolina became the ultimate rebels. Born to the highest purple of Charleston's slave-holding aristocracy, they deserted the South and invaded New England "like screaming banshees....From 1835 to 1838 they were the anguish and fury of the abolition movement, driven by inner devils that made them the most passionate of all Puritans." (Lader, 61) At a time when women were often excluded even from anti-slavery meetings, they were speaking to overflow audiences of women when men began to integrate the audiences. Describing one such incident in the Town Hall of Dorchester, Lader recounts this story: "A few men, listening through the windows, finally squeezed into the back of the hall. All that week, more and more men joined the ladies in what horrified New Englanders would soon call 'promiscuous audiences.'" Soon the sisters were speaking six nights a week to audiences in the thousands. And their message went straight to the heart.

According to Lader, while both sisters were outstanding, Angelina "wrung the deepest passions of her audience." The first feminine abolitionist in the North who had lived intimately with slavery, she "knew how to translate her own revulsion into a virtual orgy of pain and guilt. She considered herself an instrument of God. Her mission was to immerse each audience in her own neurotic suffering. They wept with her as she hit the sawdust trail in town after town, flooding New England in an ocean of tears." And further, Lader noted: "Overnight, the abolitionist crusade became a tangle of screaming, hair-pulling hellions. Garrison plunged gaily into the fray. At the annual meeting of the New England Anti-Slavery Society, he forced through a resolution allowing women to sit on the convention floor. The delegates from the Andover Theological Seminary protested vehemently. Eight orthodox clergymen resigned, seven others made written protests. 'The whole land seems aroused to the discussion of the province of woman,' Angelina exulted. The 'ultimate result,' she predicted, 'will most certainly be the breaking of every yoke ... an emancipation far more glorious than any the world has ever yet seen ...'" (Lader, 64-66).

Reviewing the insights I have gained in my brief study of this 19th century movement, I believe I've found at least some of the forces that propelled the issue from individual moral concern to mass action. It seems that the moral imperative of even a few individuals is contagious when circumstances enable them to communicate and organize around their concern. As perception of the issue expands, the moral imperative becomes overlaid with a variety of motives, and as it becomes a popular issue the movement takes on a life of its own, out of control of any individual or group. Organizations break into factions, each with its own agenda, leadership and power trip. What keeps the movement together must be a clear, simple and unequivocal statement of the goal–in this case, Abolition of Slavery. The personalities that provide such a statement are strong-willed, controversial, often abrasive types that act as gadflies and become centers around which the energy swirls into an irresistible force. It seems to me that throughout the conflicting motives and strategies it is the will and strength of a few individuals that keep the movement on target until victory of some sort is won.

Lessons For the New Abolitionists

Finally, what useful lessons can be drawn for the New Abolitionists of the 20th century? Abolition of War is much larger in scope and vastly more complex. Everything is at stake for the future of life on this planet. One might think that knowledge of the catastrophic, irreversible effects of even a limited war today, as portrayed in films like "On the Beach," "Testament," and "Threads," should be enough to put all people on the same side of the argument– that is, if they were rational beings. But such is not the case, and we find, instead, many phenomena in the movement today that parallel the struggle to abolish slavery.

First, the several stages of development are apparent, beginning with the long period of gestation up to the 1960's, when peace was only the business of Quakers and a few eccentric Methodists and Unitarians. It was even a "dirty word" in the 1950's when its advocates, like Abolitionists, were labeled "un-American." It became a national movement when Women Strike for Peace organized in 1963 opposing fallout shelters and the policy of Mutual Assured Destruction (MAD). Then came the student "Free Speech Movement," the anti-Vietnam-ers, various liberation-ers, and lastly, the professionals "for Social Responsibility." The build-up over twenty-odd years has been astounding to those of us who remember the lonely vigils of the 1930's, but so has the multiplication of issues and organizations, and, yes, motives. Coalitions come and go. "Networking" is the current trend. AND CLEARLY NO ONE IS IN CONTROL. Just as well, perhaps, but nowhere yet is there a clear and unequivocal focus to hold this diverse movement to a winning course. "Ban the Bomb," nuclear disarmament, arms control, draft resistance — all are limited to amelioration of the conditions of war, like efforts to "humanize" the condition of slaves. And they are equally ineffective. What is needed instead, judging from the past, is a clarion call for TOTAL ABOLITION OF WAR. Nothing less is adequate to present circumstances.

Where Shall We Look For the Leaders of the New Abolitionists?

So where do we look for the Garrisons, the Grimkes, the John Q. Adamses? To the religious community, one would expect, but the lesson of the 19th century is not particularly encouraging. While the moral awakening had come from religious origins, the leadership came from individuals, not institutions. The churches seemed to take a back seat, content with passing resolutions against slavery and often ostracizing their more militant members. As Lader noted: "The Reverend Theodore Parker stated, 'I am as much an outcast from society as if I were a convicted pirate.' The Reverend John Palfrey, after bringing his freed slaves North at his own expense, walked up Beacon Street, saying, 'Once I was invited to those fine houses, but now I never enter them.' 'It ostracized me as it did others...,' wrote Dr. Bowditch, 'Captain Oxnard, one of my father's old and respected friends, ...would even stare and scowl without speaking when we met ...'" (Lader, 73) "Harvard, equally a pillar of conservative Unitarianism and State

Street Commerce, did its best to stifle anti-slavery agitation," according to Lader. Charles Sumner, himself a Harvard graduate, was virtually hissed out of Cambridge, and William Ellery Channing, leader of the new Unitarianism, was prohibited by the board of his wealthy Federal Street Church from conducting prayers for an Abolitionist. Garrison, angry at his timidity, claimed that Channing "preferred to attack sin in the abstract than to deal with it personally." (Lader, 74-75)

Transcendentalists' Individualism Stopped Them From Social Action

Transcendentalists didn't come off any better than the churches, according to Aileen Kraditor in *Means and Ends in American Abolitionism*. They did not beget social action because they were "infinitely individualistic" with no means for reconciling diverse intuition. They would allow anyone's "inner voice" if only they be allowed their own. This suggests rationalizing their refusal of political responsibility and, in effect, hostility to the movement for change. Thoreau was an exception. The others assumed that all works for ultimate good without help from man, in contrast to the Abolitionists, who believed that God works through men and women and requires a struggle against sin. (Kraditor, 23-25) One is reminded of the currently popular human potential and fundamentalist movements. Again, the lesson seems to be that the crucial leadership must come from individuals, who had better not count on much support from their institutions.

The Final Stage Is the Political Arena

However well the groundwork is prepared in religious and other areas, the final stage is the political arena where the mandates of conscience are translated into law and government. For the Abolition of War this means the acceptance by national governments of world law, world courts and a limited world government. Fortunately, this is one area where the groundwork has already been laid. Laws already exist outlawing weapons of mass destruction and war itself. They have been agreed to by most national governments, including the

United States and the Soviet Union, and have even been applied, as in the Nuremberg trials of former Nazis. A world court of sorts also exists, called the International Court of Justice, located in The Hague. What does not exist is the will of national leaders to submit their differences to the rule of law instead of the rule of force. To induce them to take this step from anarchy to a civilized world order is the task ahead. It is difficult even in a democracy, where the will of the majority is not necessarily on the side of reason or of right, and where political parties, in order to win elections, must put party unity above principle.

Jacksonian democracy, believing that "The decrees of universal conscience (i.e. majority will) are the nearest approach to the Presence of God in the soul of man" did, in effect, like the transcendentalists, rationalize absence of the urge to reform in the face of the majority opposition. (Kraditor, 25) In short the lesson from the past may be that creation of a small one-issue party like the Liberty Party, or the 20th century Greens or Unity Party would serve to focus the issue and make Abolition of War politically feasible, in time, to a major convention.

The Most Important Lesson From the 19th Century is "It Can Be Done"

The most important lesson from the 19th century is that IT CAN BE DONE! In spite of all the obstacles—which are pretty much the same now as then—slavery as an institution was legally abolished. The victory was not complete—racism and discrimination remained—but it was decisive. It put the power of government and the majority on the side of reason and the now "self-evident truth." So it has happened many times before with the abolition of infanticide, cannibalism and other evils, ample evidence that war, too, can be abolished. That does not mean that conflicts among nations will end, but that they will be resolved in a civilized manner as they are now among cities and states.

The remaining question is whether abolition of war can be achieved without a worldwide war. The evidence is that it can. Slavery was abolished in the British Empire in 1833 by an act of Parliament without firing a shot, and the resolutions proposed by John

Quincy Adams to the House of Representatives could have done the same in America according to Lader (99). What is needed today is some global statesmanship on the part of political leaders, and a constituency of world-minded citizens.

It would be the ultimate irony if it took a final holocaust to make the need for abolition of war accepted, at last, as self-evident!

BIBLIOGRAPHY

Dillon, Merton L., *The Abolitionists: The Growth of a Dissenting Minority*, New York & London: W.W. Norton, 1974, 286 pp.

Hawkins, Hugh, *The Abolitionists: Immediatism and the Question of Means*, Boston: D.C. Heath & Co., 1964, 100 pp.

Kraditor, Aileen S., *Means and Ends in American Abolitionism:* "Garrison and his Critics on Strategy and Tactics, 1830-1850," New York: Pantheon Books (Random House), 1967, 296 pp.

Lader, Lawrence, *The Bold Brahmins*, New York: Dutton & Co., 1961 (2nd Ed., Westport, CT: Greenwood Press, 1973), 318 pp.

Pease, William and Jane, eds., *The Anti-Slavery Argument*, Indianapolis: Bobbs-Merrill Co., Inc., 1965 (in American Heritage Series)

Thomas, John L., ed., *Slavery Attacked: The Abolitionist Crusade*, Englewood Cliffs, NJ: Prentice Hall, Inc., 1965, 178 pp. (Spectrum Book)

PART IV

TOWARD A GOVERNED WORLD

Logo of the First Unitarian Church of Berkeley, CA

FROM INDEPENDENCE TO INTERDEPENDENCE

The year of the bicentennial celebration of the U.S. Declaration of Independence was an occasion for comparisons between 1776 and 1976. "Declarations of Interdependence" sprang up everywhere. Here I propose some values and institutions needed for the interdependent world of 1976.

On July 4th, 1976 Americans celebrated the 200th year of the signing of the Declaration of Independence. That Declaration, whose phrases still resound wherever liberty is sought, laid down the cornerstone on which the basic structure of American society has been built. The Constitution, the check-and-balance system, the Bill of Rights, the traditions of economic and religious freedom–these have been constructed upon the ideology proclaimed in the Declaration, namely, that all men are created equal and endowed with certain rights, which it is the purpose of government to secure. This idea of government as an instrument to protect the liberty and rights of the people is known as the "liberal" viewpoint, and the philosophy which derives from it "Liberalism."

Although the term "Liberalism" is currently out of favor in America, having been maligned by radicals and conservatives alike, someone should stand up in this Bicentennial Year and say "Liberal is beautiful!" For it is the style in which the edifice of American society was conceived and built. Although some aspects have taken too long to build, some are still unfinished, and others have turned out incongruous with the original vision, the basic liberalism of our legal, political and social institutions have made the American experiment possible. Without it the creation of any kind of unity out of the range

---

* *This was the sermon given at the 1st Unitarian Church of Berkeley on Memorial Day, 1976.* It was reproduced in *Dharma World*, Tokyo, 1977, Vol. 4.

that existed of diverse elements –religious, racial, cultural–would have been unattainable. The broad degree of tolerance has proved creative for almost everyone in the long run. Even latecomers in the liberation movements of today, like ethnic minorities, women and homosexuals, base their claim to equal rights on the foundations laid down by the Declaration of Independence. For "independence" is not a gift of nature, but a human achievement accomplished through the intervention of government and laws. If these were swept away in the tides of change we could be hurled back into a dark age of tyranny, or perhaps into some drab age of uniformity, where all claims to human rights and freedom would be futile.

The structures of "independence" have been creative for the past 200 years and are still to be cherished for the great achievements they embody in the advance of human dignity and welfare. But conditions are now changing which put them somewhat out of whack. For example: technology has created unforeseen problems and possibilities; industry and the environment are on a collision course; television and travel are melting the barriers that once isolated people from each other making them *interdependent*; and internationally we are locked into a nuclear arms race toward global disaster from which nobody is independent. In his State of the Union Address, January 15, 1975, President Ford said, "At no time in our peacetime history has the state of the Nation depended more heavily on the state of the world; and seldom, if ever, has the state of the world depended more heavily on the state of our Nation."

We have been catapulted by our power and knowledge into a world of new dimensions. Suddenly we realize the world is not a checkerboard of yellow, pink and purple territories on a flat chart, but a complex, organic interrelation of land, water, air, energy, and all living things. Nothing is really independent any more from anything else. So we need now to begin building new structures on the basis of new perceptions of the *interdependence* of human beings with nature and with each other.

The first step is to lay down the cornerstone with a Declaration of Interdependence. A number of such Declarations of Interdependence have been written, and several different versions were featured during the Bicentennial ceremonies in Philadelphia on July 4th.[1] One such Declaration, printed in full at the end of this paper, was drawn up and signed at the World Citizens Assembly, which had met in San Francisco the previous July on the thirtieth anniversary of the founding of the United Nations. All signers or supporters of such declarations become, in effect, world citizens committed to the building of new structures for an interdependent world.

What Are Some of the New Institutions to be Created on the Foundations of a Declaration of Interdependence?

In the political and legal area, there will grow out of the assemblies of individual world citizens (which already exist in many forms and by many names including non-governmental citizens' organizations) a constituent assembly in which delegates will represent the people who elect them, rather than a state or nation. Such a "Parliament of Man" or "House of Representatives" may or may not be added eventually to the present United Nations Assembly which, like the U.S. Senate, represents only the states.

A World Constitution must then be drafted. Notable among numerous efforts is one called, *A Constitution for the Federation of Earth.*[2] If agreement is achieved on one, it may become a substantial foundation for the rest of the political and legal structure.

---

[1] The idea of a Declaration of Interdependence is not new. The basic concept was conceived and put into writing on several occasions since the First World War. At the time of the League of Nations, Carey Thomas, first woman president of Bryn Mawr College, wrote a "Declaration of Interdependence of the World." Following the close of World War II, Will Durant wrote a Declaration that was signed in the Hollywood Bowl at the same time the United Nations was being formed. In 1956, another Declaration of Interdependence was written and signed in Philadelphia at Independence Hall on the 250th anniversary of the birth of Benjamin Franklin. In 1971, on the 26th Anniversary Memorial of the A-Bomb disaster, a Declaration of Interdependence was jointly written and signed by Japanese and American participants. In July, 1975, more than 500 concerned individuals met in a world assembly in San Francisco and signed the Declaration that appears at the end of this article. In September, 1975, the World Affairs Council of Philadephia released a Declaration of Interdependence written by Dr. Henry Steel Commager. One has also been written by the International Association for Religious Freedom in Tokyo, 1976.

[2] *A Constitution for the Federation of Earth* by the World Constitution and Parliament Association, 1974, 1480 Hoyt Street, Suite 31, Lakewood, Colorado 80215. Other constitutions for the world include: *World Constitution: Study of the Legal Framework of a World Federation* by Thomas Breitner, 1963, Berkeley, California; *A Constitution for the World* by the Center for the Study of Democratic Institutions, Santa Barbara, 1965; *Outline for a World Federation* by Shigetsugu Nakao, 1975, reprinted in the World Citizens Assembly *Report of Proceedings*, 1975.

A "Universal Declaration of Human Rights" already exists and (with some minor revisions) needs only to be incorporated into a legal system. Likewise a "Declaration on the Human Environment" was agreed to by the nations in Stockholm in 1972 and needs only the power of enforcement.

This points up the necessity of a functioning world court. The usefulness of the present one called The International Court of Justice, is limited by the "sovereign right" of each nation to submit or not to submit to its authority. In America this "right" is embodied in the Connally Amendment which says, in effect, that we will decide whether or not we will be tried! Similar reservations in other countries undercut the capacity of the court to function in international disputes. It is like a keystone without an arch. The rest of the structure must be built and the keystone put in its place.

New laws are needed to regulate the use of air, oceans and outer space, which are nominally "the common heritage of mankind." Yet there is no trustee for them except the United Nations, which does not at present represent the common good of mankind but the separate goods of separate nations. This has been painfully evident in the various environmental conferences held under U.N. auspices since 1972. On the other hand, *A Constitution for the Federation of Earth* provides for a democratic world government that would represent humankind and operate the earth's resources in the interest of all the people

And there should be a "Bill of Rights" for those who can't vote: the children, the animals, the wilderness.[3]

In the area of moral values, a form of the Golden Rule, "Do as you would be done by," should be extended beyond human relations to include all nature's creations. It becomes the duty of the individual person to act out of respect for the total environment, not just other human beings. I call this the "Ecological Imperative." (See my article, "From Territorial to Ecological Imperative" in the Uniquest publication, *Ecological Imperative*.)[4] Killing and torture of animals for fun and fur coats would be intolerable, as would wasting energy,

---

[3] See, for example, *A Wilderness Bill of Rights* by William O. Douglas. Little, Brown & Company, Canada, 1965.

[4] *Ecological Imperative* published by Uniquest Foundation, 1975. First Unitarian Church of Berkeley, 1 Lawson Road, Berkeley, California 94707.

polluting the air and water, and taking long-range chances for short-term gains in nuclear energy.

In education there must be a more integrative approach to learning than exists under the present system that has divided subject matter into "independent" departments, which behave very much like nation states. Schools cannot go on for long producing "specialty idiots" who know a lot about a single subject but little or nothing about life and how their career fits into the total scheme of things. To be relevant, education must be related organically to life in today's complex of scientific, social, moral and political aspects, and this requires an interdisciplinary, humanistic approach.

There are a few encouraging signs that point toward a global perspective in education, for example in the work of the Global Education Associates, the International Association of Educators for World Peace, and the creation of a United Nations University. The National Education Association has chosen as its theme for the Bicentennial–get this –"A Declaration of Interdependence: Education for a Global Community;" and a black educator, speaking to a multicultural workshop sponsored by the California State Department of Education, said that "Ethnic studies should have goals that are more consistent with the needs of a global society. Events within the last decade have dramatically indicated that we live in a world society that is beset with momentous social and human problems, many of which are related to ethnic hostility and conflict....It is imperative that the school...play a decisive role in educating citizens who have both the vision and the courage to make our world more humane."[5]

To accomplish this, more emphasis must be placed on cultivation of the emotional and intuitive aspects of learning (the "right" hemisphere of the brain according to Robert Ornstein), which has been neglected in our concentration on logical, rational and practical aspects. The techniques of sensitivity training and oriental disciplines such as yoga and meditation can be used in the classroom to more advantage in developing the whole, integrated person.

Finally, it seems that a clearer realization is emerging of the interdependence of the "outer worlds," from macrocosm to micro-

---

[5] James A. Banks in *The Post*, May 12, 1976, p. 3.

cosm, with the "inner worlds" of spiritual consciousness. Like concentric spheres carved by some ancient Chinese artist, they move one inside the other, inseparable and yet, in a way, "free." Their freedom consists not in their independence, but in their ability to move in harmony with each other. How many of these concentric spheres there may be, we can only guess as we look deeper into outer space and inner space. Perhaps the limits are only those of our present vision. But we can now begin to understand that freedom is not independence from one or the other, but harmony within and among these worlds.

This kind of freedom, like the other, is not a natural condition but a human achievement. The possibility is present in the original clay, but the actualizing of free, harmonious movement must be carved out with skill, imagination and patience by human artists. To move fluently from inner to outer space is an accomplishment of the mind and spirit. And today nothing less will do. We are like the Bodhisattvas who would not be "free" until the last blade of grass is free. To free the grass and all nature and thereby ourselves –at least from our own mischief–requires the creating of laws and other institutions for an interdependent world community. The hunters and trappers, the baby seal coats, the litter, the famine, the nuclear stockpiles will not *just go away*. They will have to be *made to go*.

This is the task now before all world citizens–to build the necessary structures of a world community. As the Declaration of 1776 began an independent, self-governing society committed to securing certain rights and freedoms for individual citizens, may the Declarations of 1976 begin an interdependent, self-governing global society committed to securing survival, in harmonious interaction, for all of its inhabitants.

𝔇eclaration 𝔒f 𝔍nterdependence·

WE THE UNITED PEOPLE OF THE WORLD DETERMINED:

𝕿𝕺 *save succeeding generations from the scourge of war . . .*
𝕿𝕺 *insure fundamental human rights . . .*
𝕿𝕺 *unite our strength to guarantee world peace . . .*
𝕿𝕺 *promote social progress, better standards of life and freedom . . .*
𝕿𝕺 *live together in peace as good neighbors . . . (Preamble to United Nations Charter)*

𝖂𝖊 *THE UNITED PEOPLE OF THE WORLD are aware that we are entering upon a new era in the evolution of humankind. Out of deep respect for the dignity, freedom and interdependence of all humankind, we reaffirm the truth that differences of race, color, sex, age, religious and political beliefs are natural; that diverse groups, institutions, and ideas are stimulating elements for the creative development of humankind; and that to generate unity in diversity is the responsibility and challenge before men and women throughout the world.*

𝖂𝖊 *THE UNITED PEOPLE OF THE WORLD urge all to join in cooperative action:*
To advance human fellowship through mutual trust, understanding and harmony;
To champion the uniqueness of the person, human dignity, and universal rights;
To strive together to discourage hostility, exclusiveness, and aggressiveness;
To foster an enlightening synthesis through education, planning, human encounter, and service;
To build with joy a world civilization based on freedom, justice, and peace founded on reverence for life;
To insure that all factors of humankind and nature are returned to balance for the health,. welfare, good, and happiness of all;
To provide present and future generations with the opportunity for maximum realization of their potential.

𝖂𝖊 *THE UNITED PEOPLE OF THE WORLD, recognizing our common sacred origin, facing a world in crisis, to insure our survival and fulfillment, HAVE RESOLVED TO COMBINE OUR EFFORTS, form a movement to unite the people of the world, elect delegates to a world assembly, and establish world institutions that give the people of the world control of their own destiny.*

* *As written and adopted by the participants in the first World Citizens Assembly in San Francisco on July 25, 1975.*

93

Logo of the Federalist Caucus

POSITIVE STEPS TOWARD PERMANENT PEACE

In the "race between reality and doomsday" steps are proposed to close the "Reality Gap," the cause of psychic numbing from the incredible facts of the arms race. Elements of a world community that are already in existence are identified–along with some that still remain to be created.

Since the first atomic bomb was dropped on Hiroshima, most people have been unable to face the enormity of the danger or take effective action against it. It was not lack of knowledge, for the awful effects of nuclear weapons have been well documented since 1945. It was the inability to digest the reality of it that made so many hide their heads while the Bomb expanded into stockpiles equivalent to over 1,300,000 Hiroshima-size weapons ready to go off at the touch of a button. These were accepted by many as a kind of security blanket along with the soothing "doctrine of deterrence." Only in the last few years have people aroused themselves in enough numbers to get serious attention from their governments and the press. This "primal rebellion of the mind against psychic numbing and toward reality" may accelerate realistic and constructive action as time goes on, as predicted by Yale psychiatrist, Dr. Robert Lifton, but it is truly "a race between reality and doomsday."[1] This rebellion toward reality comes none too soon.

The Reality Gap has existed since 1945. Albert Einstein said, "The unleashed power of the atom has changed everything save our modes of thinking, and thus we drift toward unparalleled catastrophe... a new type of thinking is essential if mankind is to survive and move toward higher levels." He added, "with all my heart I believe

---

1 Quoted from a speech delivered to Physicians for Social Responsibility, in the *San Francisco Chronicle*, January 22, 1983, p.8.

that the world's present system of sovereign nations can lead to barbarism, war, and inhumanity, and only through world law can we assure progress toward civilization, peace, and humanity." [2] The size and nature of atomic weapons disqualify them for defending a border or one select group of people against another. Their indiscriminate effects render obsolete the ability of "independent" nations in competition with each other to secure the health and safety of their citizens. "National security," becomes meaningless in this interdependent world, and the persistence of the idea of "national sovereignty" (that is, every nation is a law-unto-itself) makes terrorists of national leaders and hostages of all the people.

At the same time photographs from space show the view of Earth as one blue-and-white planet without dotted lines marking blotches of pink, yellow and purple called "national territories." It should be clear from space as well as from other technologies (communications, commerce, energy and of course, weaponry) that this is, in fact, one planet and that we human inhabitatns will perish—if we perish—not as separate nations but as one human family along with our animal and plant relations, and that we will survive—if we survive—as one blue-and-white planet, not a crazy-quilt of pink, yellow and purple blotches surrounded by dotted lines.

To close the Reality Gap it is not enough to wake up to the monstrosity of the arms race as many have done, although that may be a beginning. It is a hopeful sign that the nuclear freeze initiatives received overwhelming support in the 1982 elections and that polls conducted in the United States, Canada and elsewhere regularly show a two-to-one majority in favor of nuclear disarmament. That is a start in the right direction, but it is not a solution to the problem. The nightmare world is still there with its over-kill, its balance of terror, its push-button timing, its first-strike mentality and illusion of a "winnable" nuclear war. The nightmare itself is real, incredible as it seems, and it will not go away until its cause is eliminated. That cause is anarchy among competing sovereign nations armed with nuclear

---

2 Quoted in an article on Einstein's 100th anniversary in *World Citizen*, Vol. 6, No. 1, Spring 1979, p.5.

weapons. The old system of independent nations is obsolete. A new system has not yet evolved for realistic management of the Earth's affairs, especially for keeping the peace. Meanwhile, the Earth totters precariously on the brink of disaster.

It is not enough, either, to look to the United Nations. Although it was organized in 1945 "to save succeeding generations from the scourge of war," it has evolved into an instrument for preserving the anachronism of "independent" states in an increasingly interdependent world. It is thereby extending the Reality Gap. The practice of one-nation-one-vote in the General Assembly, where member nations range in population from 60,000 (Seychelles) to 1,000,000,000 (China), underscores the unreality in human terms. The veto power of each of the five biggest nations in the Security Council renders that institution ineffective in practical terms for averting major wars, although it has served as an arbiter in some minor ones. The failure of the U.N. Special Session on Disarmament in 1982 to achieve any significant agreement on action was "The final confirmation of the bankruptcy of the existing international system as exemplified in the U.N." according to Richard Hudson, Editor of *Disarmement Times*. [3] While the United Nations has its usefulness in some specialized areas, as a "last, best hope of peace" it is not promising, nor will it be without drastic structural reform.

What is needed, then, to close the Reality Gap and change this nightmare world into a healthy, functioning community? A community is not a utopia; its members need not be especially virtuous or love one another. They *do* need to be organized in such a way that they do not kill each other over their differences and can accomplish the work necessary to their collective survival. A world community need not be a paradise or a "Kingdom of God,"; it does need realistic structures for intelligent problem-solving on a global level. Such structures have been tested throughout history on a smaller scale within cities, counties and states and found to work, creating stable, civilized communities in spite of the imperfections of human nature. The

3 In *Disarmament Times*, Vol. V, No. 22, 13 July, 1982, p. 1

lesson to be applied is that we need not await some mystical transformation of human nature in order to create a civilized world order that works. We need to extend to the global arena the tools found essential to community life–tools for rational decision-making and conflict-resolution.

Some prerequisites to a world community already exist. For example, the technology for global communication is in place; world trade operates in spite of international anarchy; and there is a growing awareness of common destiny among people of different nations as manifested in the worldwide peace movement. Yet the world is not "working." Two-thirds of the human family lack basic necessities of food and shelter; our environmental housekeeping is a mess; and the wealth and resources needed to solve both problems go up the chimney at a rate of $6,000,000,000 a year, fueled by the arms race.

What Does it Take to Make this World Community Work?

Two factors remain to be created: **first**, a global institution for decision-making based on real-life values (people and the environment) instead of – or at least in addition to – the fictions of national "interest," national "independence" and national "security" now represented in the United Nations; and, **second**, a global system of law and courts as a compulsory alternative to war. Where these factors exist, as in democratic federal government, peace is the normal condition. Where they do not, as in tyranny or anarchy, war and oppression are inevitable. Knowing this, national leaders are understandably reluctant to give up their arms, which they see as protecting whatever security they possess, until and unless there are global alternatives to war. Thus, general and complete disarmament is likely to follow, not precede world order. (This is a lesson that anti-nuclear activists have yet to learn).

How can such institutions possibly come into being? Fortunately, beginnings have been made toward both, although they are not well-known to people in the disarmament movement. For example, several proposals are in the works for democratizing the United Nations: by direct election of delegates in countries where that is possible, by "weighted voting" according to population and other factors, and by creation of a People's Assembly in which people and non-government organizations (NGO's) can participate in deliberations at the General Assembly in New York.

Especially noteworthy is the development of a new international network of elected legislators (over 600 from 25 countries according to The Federalist Caucus report for 1982) called "Parliamentarians Global Action," that coordinates legislative initiatives in their respective governments. One such initiative is the "Call for Global Survival" signed by 500 parliamentarians representing 50 million people around the world. It calls for an immediate freeze on nuclear arsenals to be followed by an eventual international system providing "true security" through such measures as: disarmament by all nations to the level required for internal security; an international inspection organization able to monitor disarmament using both satellites and on-sight inspection; a world peace force able to enforce disarmament and prevent international aggression; an effective system of world courts and tribunals; and a world development fund through which resources saved could help the poorest nations. Their first "U.N. Parliamentary Forum" held in September, 1981, "laid a solid foundation for an expanded role for parliamentarians in the U.N. system, which could in turn make a major contribution toward strengthening, democratizing and invigorating the world organization," according to its chairman, Douglas Roche, M.P. of Canada.

Far more radical was the First Session of a Provisional World Parliament convened in September, 1982 in Brighton, England calling for "people who want to survive to take charge of world affairs." It was convened under *A Constitution for the Federation of the Earth*, which had been created over a period of twenty years by an international group of world citizens. This Parliament represented a constituency of 4 million people across national boundaries through elected delegates coming from two dozen different countries, with the largest delegations from India, Nigeria, the U.S.A. and Canada. Included were M.P.'s from national parliaments, former prime ministers and cabinet ministers, lawyers, doctors, judges, businessmen, writers, professors, and leaders of women's movements each acting in the name of people rather than governments. This gave the

Parliament a very different complexion from the United Nations. (It is worth noting that in numbers represented, the Parliament was larger than half of the nations represented in the U.N. Assembly, and that the delegates were more democratically elected than U.N. delegates, who are appointed by their governments, many of which are military dictatorships). In the two-week session, foundations were laid for a continuing peoples parliament that will meet on a regular basis until a permanent democratic, federal world government is established according to provisions in the *Constitution for the Federation of Earth*. Significantly, the first legislative action of the Provisional World Parliament in September was to pass unanimously Bill Number One, "To outlaw nuclear weapons and other weapons of mass destruction and to create a world disarmament agency." This was followed by a World Court Bill for the establishment of provisional district world courts to adjudicate issues arising from this and other world laws. The first such extra-national court is established in Los Angeles, ready to try cases and to issue injunctions and citations for violations of existing world law. Other similar courts are expected to follow suit.[4]

This action, while it may seem quixotic in the face of overwhelming powers like the military-industrial complex, gives added impetus to legal actions by private groups based on a substantial body of world laws in existence, ratified by governments, defining "crimes" against humanity and peace including the use or threat to use weapons of mass destruction. These laws are being compiled into briefs by various groups of lawyers to be used in judicial actions against the agents of governments. [5] Such action publicizes the existence of world law, which most people are unaware of and which most governments choose to ignore, and it creates the possibility of a system of extra-national or supra-national world courts, the second of two factors needed to make the world community work. The foundations for world law that have already been laid are impressive

---

4 Contact Leon Vickman Law Corporation, 16255 Ventura Blvd., Suite 605, Encino, CA 91436

5 For examples: The Lawyers Committee on Nuclear Policy, 225 Lafayette St., Suite 207, new York, NY 10012; Court of Man Foundation, Inc., 9595 Wilshire Blvd., Beverly Hills, CA 90210; Judicial Action Committee of the World Federalist of Canada, c/o David Winninger, Lawyer, #301, 483 Richmond St., London, Ontario N6A3E4, Canada; and Lawyers v. The Bomb, 2 Garden Court, Temple, London EC4, England.

(See also a previous article, "To Outlaw War Altogether").

It is clear that the engines of the military-industrial complex ride roughshod over these fragile structures of peace and will continue to do so until there is a force strong enough to stop them. But foundations have been laid for a civilized world order. Two remaining requirements for a functional world community exist at least in part: a democratic body for decision-making based on real-life values, and a system of laws and courts for conflict-resolution without war. They need only the allegiance of enough people to make them work. The Reality Gap is closing, but will the aroused public move beyond protest and disarmament to take the positive steps needed to build a permanent peace?

Logo of the U.S. Bicentennial Celebrations in Philadelphia

OUR CONSTITUTIONAL CONVENTION:
REHEARSAL FOR WORLD FEDERATION

Anticipating the Bicentennial of the U.S. Constitutional Convention in 1989, this paper presented to the Outlook Club of Berkeley the striking parallels between the situation at the time of the U.S. Confederacy and the predicament of the United Nations today. Inspired by Carl Van Doren's book, The Great Rehearsal, it proceeds to recount the development of constitutional federal government throughout the world from the U.S. model to the European Community. But where – with America now flawed by scandals – can the leading roles come from for the final act of transformation to a world federation?

In 1945, Emery Reves had just finished writing *The Anatomy of Peace* outlining the structures needed to maintain a peaceful world when the atomic bomb was dropped on Hiroshima. He wrote a postscript to his book predicting what would happen under the United Nations as long as it remained an association in which each state continues a law unto itself or retained, in other words, its national "sovereignty." Each great power will always do its utmost to lead in military science, he said, and "The people of the world must understand the forces driving them toward the coming holocaust. It has nothing whatever to do with Communism or Capitalism, with individualism or collectivism. It is the inevitable conflict between nonintegrated sovereignties in contact. We could put a Communist in the White House or establish the purest Jeffersonian democracy in Russia and the situation would be the same. Unless an overall world government organization can be established in time by persuasion and consent, no diplomatic magic will prevent the explosion."

From a speech delivered at the Outlook Club, Berkeley, CA, March 17, 1988 and printed that year in *Worldview Perspective* for the 20th anniversary of the Academy of World Studies, San Francisco.

Parallels Between 1787 and 1987

Then, in 1947, Carl Van Doren wrote of a different scenario that could happen if lessons were learned from the U.S. Constitutional Convention of 1787. The name of his book was *The Great Rehearsal: The Story of the Making and Ratifying of the Constitution of the United States*. While the parallels between 1787 and 1947 are naturally not exact, he says, "it is impossible to read the story of the making and ratifying of the Constitution of the United States without finding there all the arguments in favor of a general government for the United Nations, as well as all the arguments now raised in opposition to it." For some examples:

Opponents of the Constitution argued in 1787 that the United States was too large to be held together by a common government, and that any government strong enough to dominate the whole country would be a tyrannical super-state with no respect for the liberty of individual citizens. Supporters argued that the larger a federation the less chance that one part would dominate the others, and that it would be designed and administered by officers chosen by the people and subject to control or change at the will of the people.

Opponents insisted that smaller states would be swallowed up, and that larger states "would disturb the union by their contentions." Supporters pointed out that small states, always vulnerable in isolation, would find security in union with friendly states, and that larger states would be more likely, under a union, to arrive at peaceable agreements.

Opponents were convinced that citizens could only be protected by their separate sovereign states. Supporters "knew that conflicting sovereignties had been the causes of most wars in which the people have regularly suffered."

Opponents could talk only of the difficulties of forming a new government. **Supporters,** aware of the dangers facing the Confederacy, demanded that the attempt be made no matter what the difficulties.

"In this respect," concludes Carl Van Doren, "those antagonists were precisely like the enemies and friends of world federation in 1948, now when it is obvious that no difficulty in the way of world government can match the danger of a world without it .... the supporters of the Constitution in 1787 knew that they were planning a government only for the United States, but they believed their experiment would instruct and benefit all mankind. Their undertaking might be, though of course no one of them ever used the term, a rehearsal for the federal governments of the future." (Van Doren, Preface)

Poignant Similarities

There are poignant similarities between the periods leading up to 1787 and to 1987. Both began with victories in war — but victories that led not to union and peace, but to confusion and anarchy. The spirit of cooperation that had won the wars disintegrated under the pressures of competing independent states. In the 18th century under the Articles of Confederation, there were, for example, trade rivalries among all thirteen states, and territorial disputes in which thousands of people lost their lives. New York and New Jersey shot it out in the harbor over the right to tax incoming ships. Pennsylvania and New Jersey could not agree on a border. The value of a citizen's currency would shrink 10 percent whenever crossing a state line, so that a person starting from New Hampshire with $100 would have only $20 left by the time he reached Georgia without having spent a cent. Each state was minting its own money. Some would not even accept the money of other states. Tariff barriers were erected. There were sharp differences in religion, customs, and language. Pennsylvania had declared German to be its official language. A farmers' rebellion erupted in Massachusetts. Two thousand people lost their lives in a war over their rights in the Wyoming Valley in Pennsylvania.

The Continental Congress was impotent in dealing with such problems, for it had no power to enforce its laws, no independent taxing power, and required unanimous vote for any amendments. These weaknesses, among others of the Confederacy, are weaknesses of the United Nations today.

Views in 1787: The People, Morris and Randolph

When the Constitutional Convention was called in 1787 to strengthen the Articles of Confederation, public opinion of "the man on the street" was described thus: "Both in Philadelphia and elsewhere there were many more who were uninformed or indifferent as to any need of change; a good many were jealous for the sovereignty of their separate states; some who feared that a stronger federal constitution might create a superstate in which local self-government would be lost; a few who had come to the conclusion that people of so widespread a confederation could never govern themselves." (Van Doren, 21)

Delegates to the Convention from New Jersey, Delaware and Massachusetts came with specific instructions to limit discussion to amending the old Charter, as the Convention had been authorized to do. But Gouverneur Morris of Pennsylvania objected, saying that a federal government should have a right to compel every part to do its duty. States and federal governments cannot both be supreme. We must have one government or none. He added, "We had better take a supreme government now, than a despot twenty years hence–for come he must in the anarchy that will result from the present confusion." (Ibid, 33)

Governor Randolph of Virginia spoke early in the Convention about the need for an adequate government and the defects of the Articles of Confederation. Noteworthy are the parallels to problems of the United Nations today. He said:

(1) "An adequate government must be able to secure the country against foreign invasion." Congress under the Articles could not do

that because it could not control individual states in their relations with foreign countries.

(2) "An adequate government must be able to prevent dissentions among the states or seditions in them. Congress had neither constitutional right nor sufficient force to do these things."

(3) "An adequate government must be able to provide for general benefits, such as regulation of interstate trade, development of national works ... (etc.) which individual states could not accomplish alone." The Articles had no means or authority to provide the people with such 'blessings.'"

(4) "An adequate government must be able to defend itself against the encroachments of the several states." The history of the Confederation had been full of steady resistance by the states to federal measures.

(5) "An adequate central government must be superior to local governments." Under the Articles there was no federal constitution paramount to the state constitutions either in law or effect. (Ibid, 31)

The Virginia Plan Versus The New Jersey Plan

Governor Randolph then presented the Virginia plan which he and his colleagues had drawn up in advance. Debate ensued between the New Jersey plan, which was basically for states rights, and the Virginia plan. The differences were described this way:

"Supporters of the New Jersey plan, strict in their interpretation of the instructions, found arguments in the sovereign rights of the separate states. The supporters of the Virginia plan, creative in their interpretation, found arguments in the rights of all the American people to a general government which could furnish them the peace, liberty and security they had not found under the Confederation. The New Jersey plan was in the interest of the separate states. The Virginia plan was in the interest of the united people." (Ibid, 91)

There followed a great debate between the two and, as now well known, the Virginia position eventually emerged after much discussion and many compromises.

Differences Seemed Irreconcilable

Many differences seemed irreconcilable: regional ones between east and west, north and south, between the interests of large states and small ones, industrialized and agricultural, between "free" and slave, and between those concerned with the rights of the individual and those concerned with the rights of the state. Pierce Butler of South Carolina wrote home that the interest of Southern and Eastern states were "as different as the interests of Russia and Turkey." What did Connecticut know about growing rice or indigo? What did Pennsylvania know about an economy based on slave labor? Even James Madison, comparatively well informed, admitted that he knew as little about the affairs of Georgia as of Kamchatka. Thomas Jefferson once wrote a friend about the character of the states:

In the North, they are:	In the South, they are:
cool	fiery
sober	voluptuary
laborious	indolent
persevering	unsteady
independent	zealous of their own liberties
jealous of their liberties & those of others	but trampling on those of others
chicaning	generous
superstitious & hypocritical in in their religion	candid
	without attachment or pretensions to any religion but that of the heart.
	(Bowen, 92)

Compromises Made Federal Union Possible - But One Compromise Had Tragic Consequenses

"The Great Compromise," as it was called, was achieved between the large states, which wanted voting by population, and the states which wanted to retain the advantage of one state-one vote. It was done by creating both a House of Representatives (at that time called the "First House") which appealed to the large states because of representation by population, and a Senate, in which each state had equal representation which satisfied the small states. Other compromises were made between the industrial North and agricultural South and between the free states and the slave states. *(The latter, involving an extra three-fifths vote by the owner for each slave that he owned, resulted in a House so dominated by slave-owners that emancipation could not be achieved by parliamentary means, as in other countries. Perhaps the Union would never have been achieved without it, but that one compromise had tragic results.)* The innovation of a check-and-balance system among the three branches of government: Legislative, Executive and Judicial, was another compromise with those who feared some sort of "tyranny." And, finally, when the complete Constitution included no bill of rights, Anti-Federalists saw a plot. Had not the Convention insisted on secrecy throughout four entire months? They complained that, "The evil genius of darkness presided at the Constitution's birth. It came forth under the veil of mystery." So a Bill of Rights was added in 1789. (Ibid, 273)

A Government, Formed Out of Discordant and Uncompromising Material, Quickly Ratified, Brought Peace

Catherine Drinker Bowen in *Miracle in Philadelphia* wrote, "It is significant that when the Convention adjourned in September and the Constitution was made public, members expressed themselves as astonished at what they had achieved. Washington declared it was 'much to be wondered at ... little short of a miracle.' Charles Pinckney told his fellow Carolinians they should be 'astonishingly pleased' that a government 'so perfect could have been formed from such discordant and uncompromising material.'" (Ibid, 213)

Let's Abolish War and Build a World Community

None-the-less, the Constitution was signed on September 17, 1787, and within a year it had been ratified by eleven of the thirteen states. Two of the last states to ratify were the largest ones, New York and Virginia. North Carolina delayed, but came in later. Rhode

Island, when all the others had ratified, was threatened with economic isolation, saw the handwriting on the wall and came in. In March, 1789, the United States of America was in business. And now, two hundred years later, its constitution is the longest living federal constitution in the world. In has brought peace and prosperity, with the exception of the Civil War, among its states. At a Celebration in Philadelphia on July 4, 1788, it was exuberantly proclaimed: "The Union would bring peace among the states. It had been made by the people themselves, in their own right, for their own purposes. 'May reason,' said one of the toasts at Union Green, 'and not the sword, hereafter decide all national disputes.' And the people went further and drank to 'The whole Family of Mankind." (Van Doren, 250)

Many Of the Founding Fathers Thought of Themselves as World Citizens

It is evident that a number of the founding fathers of the U.S. Constitution thought of themselves as world citizens, members of "The Whole Family of mankind." They also thought of the Constitution as a model for the whole human race. For example, George Washington had come to think of himself as, in his own words, "a citizen of the great republic of humanity at large." (Van Doren, 84) He wrote to a friend in 1788, "It is a flattering and consolatory reflection, that our rising Republics have the good wishes of all the philosophers, patriots and virtuous men of all nations and that they look upon them as a kind of asylum for mankind. God grant that we may not disappoint their honest expectations, by our folly or perverseness." (Ibid, 239) Gouverneur Morris of Pennsylvania came to the convention, in his own words, "in some degree as a representative of the whole human race; for the whole human race will be affected by the proceedings of this convention." (Ibid, 112) Benjamin Franklin, in 1787, wrote to a friend in Paris, "I do not see why you might not in Europe carry the project of good Henry the Fourth into execution, by forming a Federal Union and One Grand Republic of all the different states and kingdoms, by means of a like Convention, for we had many interests to reconcile." (Ibid, 164) And again, a year later he wrote to David Hertley, "God grant, that not only the love of liberty, but a thorough knowledge of the Rights of Man, may pervade all the nations of the earth, so that a philosopher may set his foot anywhere on its surface, and say, 'This is my country.'" (Ibid, 239)

The U.S. Constitution's Influence in Creating Other Federal Systems

In fact, the U.S. Constitution embodying the federal principle for uniting states and peoples under a central government with explicitly defined powers above the state governments, has had influence in the creation of other federal systems. Dr. Joseph Baratta, historian and former United Nations representative for the World Federalists, lists at least seventeen, roughly in the chronological order of their first federal constitutions:

Argentina (1816, 1829, 1853, 1880)
Mexico (1814, 1821, 1857, 1917)
Brazil (1822, 1891)
Venezuela (1830, 1864)
Switzerland (1848)
Germany (1866, 1871, 1919, 1949)
Canada (1867)
Austria-Hungary (1867)
Australia (1901)
Yugoslavia (1918, 1953)
Austria (1920, 1953)
Czechoslovakia (1920, 1948, 1960)
USSR (1922, 1936, 1977)
India (1949)
Pakistan (1956, 1962)
Malaya (1957) and Malaysia (1963)
Nigeria (1960)

In addition, there are a number of strictly unitary states that have had, or recently been given, federalist features: Union of South Africa (1910), Italy (1948), Burma (1948), China (1949), Ethiopia and Eritrea (1952), Tanzania (1964), Belgium (1980), Spain (1982). Lastly, he lists a group of "nascent federations," such as regional associations of states like the Organization of American States (1948), the Non-Aligned Movement (1961), and the Organization of African Unity (1963). (From the *World Federalist Bicentennial Reader*, 132-133)

A historical account of the creation of some of these federal systems can be found from Vernon Nash's *The World Must Be Governed* (Ibid, 83-86.) Analysis of eight of these federal constitutions (for Switzerland, USA, Canada, Australia, USSR, India, the Federal Republic of Germany and the European Community) can be found in Charlotte Waterlow's *Federal Constitutions for a Divided World*, along with some of their distinctive features.

For example, Switzerland became a modern federal state in 1848 when the 23 tribal "cantons," many of which dated back to the middle ages, surrendered some sovereignty to a Federal Government. Medieval and modern aspects are combined in maintaining the distinction of groups—linguistic and religious—along with direct democracy achieved through local assemblies and referenda on matters great and small, like joining the United Nations (which it has not done), driving on Sundays, or letting women vote (finally approved in 1971).

Canada and Australia both follow the British model with a Senate representing the provinces and a House of Commons elected on a population basis. Both had problems uniting across vast, sparsely inhabited territories with cultural differences. The story is told that when Australia was building its first transcontinental railway, each province built different gauge tracks, necessitating transfer of trains at each border. It took a federal government to make the transcontinental railway "work."

The Soviet federal constitution seeks to blend the revealed truths of Marxism with modern secular ideas of the rule of law and human rights. It also encompasses a vast range of territory as well as ethnic and linguistic variety. The Supreme Soviet has two chambers, one representing the country on a population basis and the other on the basis of regions and republics. Each of the fifteen Republics has its own constitution with the right to conduct its own diplomatic relations with other countries. (Some have separate seats in the United

Nations.) But the central government has some exclusive powers which in western federal systems are normally shared with the component states, such as direction of the country's economic and social policy and control over natural resources and economic plans.

India, the Third World's major democratic federation, contains nearly a quarter of the world's population. Seventy-five per cent of the people live in villages, with wide diversity in language and sharp contrasts in religion and race. Its federalism has to be tight and centralized in order to prevent splitting the country into separate states. Also for economic reasons the planning is centrally controlled, though not dictatorial–a social democracy, based on the implementation of social as well as civil and political rights. It also provides for universal male and female suffrage.

The Developing European Federation–Revelant to World Federation

The latest and most interesting development toward federation is in the European Community and perhaps the most relevant of all to the goal of a world federation. Its separate states had engaged for centuries in wars with each other and it was the origin and battlefield of two world wars. After World War II, many Europeans felt that a federal Europe offered the only constructive solution to the problem of Germany. There were economic motives also–and pressure from the United States to create a bastion against the Soviet Union. A Council of Europe was set up in 1948 by ten of the "democratic" states. It was without supra-national powers, but it had a useful role in creating a European consciousness with cooperation in economic and social areas. A unique achievement was to set up the European Court of Human Rights, the only one in the world where citizens can appeal over the heads of their governments. (All member states except Greece have agreed to accept the Court's verdicts as final and binding.) However, failure of the Council to create a "United States of Europe" caused the French wine merchant, Jean Monnet, to promote a gradual step-by-step approach–a kind of creeping or "functional" federalism in the least sensitive areas of public life. He called it "building community."

113

What began by placing the whole of Franco-German coal and steel output under a common High Authority developed by 1967 into the "European Community," which now consists of twelve states including Britain, Greece, Spain and Portugal. Its structure involves a Council of Ministers representing the national governments and the European Parliament which has been directly elected since 1979 by the citizens of all the member nations. Significantly, the delegates to the Parliament do not sit by nations. Instead they sit together according to philosophical orientation virtually as European parties. Within the last five years the European Community has approached closer to a Federation of Europe:

(1) By member nations agreeing to abide by majority vote rather than consensus (which, as has been seen, gives a veto to every state),

(2) By working to abolish trade and other barriers between states, and

(3) By creating a common defense and foreign policy (not always to the liking of the United States), and

(4) By also increasing the power of the Parliament in budgetary and policy-making matters.

Noteworthy is the fact that for the last forty years there has not been a single war between European states, and the possibility of one between France and Germany now seems as remote as between California and Nevada.

The European Community Is a Model for Federation

In her conclusion, (1987) Charlotte Waterlow points out, "In the 1930's, the federation of west Europe was unthinkable ... yet in the short post-war period ... the foundations of this completely new kind of federation have been solidly laid. It is hard to envision that the Community could now be unscrambled back into completely sovereign states. A great leap forward is now required to build the edifice. Meanwhile, the Community provides a model for other regions where the need for federalism is or will be felt."

"The Community has an association with 65 African, Caribbean and Pacific states, former colonies of Community members, which is institutionalized in an Executive Council of Ministers of the 12 EC members and 65 associates, and a similar Parliamentary body. They confer in these bodies about trade and aid as equal partners; and through this Association as well as by other means, understanding of the Community's complex and subtle structure is spreading to the developing world. World federalism could develop in a creeping way as a Community of Communities." (Waterlow, 40-41)

In all of these federations, creeping or not, which unite diverse elements under a central government with limited but adequate power to act for the common good, war has been replaced in settling disputes among its members by civilized instruments such as laws, courts, votes, and government (in most cases of, by and for the people). If our U.S. Constitutional Convention was a "Great Rehearsal," then these ensuing federations are scenes in a global drama whose last act will quite probably be a showdown between World Federation and the furies of modern war.

Past Leaders Could Not Imagine the Current State of the World or the Present U.S. Role In It

Our Founding Fathers could not have imagined two hundred years ago, even in their wildest nightmares, the scope and power of their antagonist in this final showdown. Nor could Emery Reves have predicted, forty years ago, that the bomb that fell on Hiroshima would mushroom into a global arsenal equivalent to two million such bombs poised to destroy life on this whole planet fifty times over. Who could foresee (or admit) that the madness of the arms race would actually be fueled by the corporate ethic of freedom for profit-at-any-price? Or that the United Nations as a confederacy would, in spite of its considerable accomplishments, be hopelessly inadequate to restrain the furies of greed and power? Saddest of all, how would our Founding Fathers feel to know that their beloved United States of America, which they expected would be hero and protagonist in this global drama, had been so corrupted by a military-industrial complex that important foreign policy could be conducted in secret by the head of the CIA, an admiral of the Navy, a general of the Air Force, and a colonel in the Marines?

The Glorification of Military Values in America

The reputation of the United States as a champion of world law, promoter of human rights and refuge of the "huddled masses yearning to breathe free" has been tarnished by repeated scandals. Rightly or wrongly, America is considered more an "outlaw" than law-giver in much of the world community today–a symbol of Machiavellian self-interest. If facts and figures are needed to document the extent of militarism in America, they are provided in *The Defense Monitor*, a periodical published independently by retired high-ranking military officers concerned about the threat to American values and the danger of nuclear war. They pointed out (in 1986, Vol. XV, Number 3) that "The glorification of military values in the United States distorts our foreign and domestic policy and raises serious concerns for the future of the democratic process in a stable, productive society." For example, close to 70% of every federal dollar allotted for Research and Development goes to the military establishment. Since 1981, overall military research spending has increased by 62% above inflation, while funding for civilian research has decreased by 10%. Massive amounts are spent on secret so-called "black" projects. The 1987 Department of Defense budget request included 22 billion dollars, a 300% increase in black funding since 1981. Total military-related funding reached $400 billion in 1987.

"The increasing influence of the military is reflected in American society. War and military solutions are glorified through movies, magazines, TV, toys, new leisure activities, and a fascination for paramilitary weapons and training," they warn. Sales of war toys in the U.S. have increased 600% since 1982, making roughly five such toys for every child. Each child is also exposed to 250 cartoons with war themes and 800 television ads for war toys a year. By the age of sixteen, each one will have watched some 20,000 hours of TV, taking in 200,000 acts of violence and 50,000 attempted murders–33,000 of which will involve guns.

America is the largest producer of firearms in the world and has the weakest gun control laws of any western democracy. The number of people licensed to sell machine guns has tripled since 1980 and there are, besides, 500,000 unregistered military-style assault guns owned in the United States. According to the FBI, sixteen American survivalist camps now provide "differing programs to include firearms, martial arts, survivalist techniques and paramilitary training." Paramilitary, survivalist and mercenary camps are presently operating in at least eleven states.

In summary, Jerome Weisner, Science adviser to Kennedy and Eisenhower, said in 1986, "It's no longer a question of controlling a military-industrial complex, but rather of keeping the United States from becoming a totally military culture." (Op. Cit., 3)

Can Civil Law and Democracy Survive Brutal Competition in An Ungoverned World?

Perhaps it is inevitable that the niceties of civil law and democracy cannot survive brutal competition in an ungoverned world and, as Athenian democracy degenerated in the wars with Sparta, so American ideals and innocence were compromised in the cold war with Russia. Ideals seem pallid in the shadow of a mushroom cloud. But what benefits a nation to "win" a nuclear war and lose whatever there was to fight for? Is America too flawed by its struggle in the aftermath of Hiroshima to be a hero in the coming global drama? (There is still hope that it is not–all the more reason to work for a governed world!)

But if it is so flawed, then who can be the protagonist?

The answer must be the people, wherever they may be, who inherit the ideals of the Founding Fathers. They are in Switzerland, in Canada and Australia, in India, Pakistan, Malaysia, Nigeria, and yes, in the USSR and USA–citizens of the world still working to build a world of peace, justice and freedom for all humanity.

What Is Their Inheritance?

And what is their inheritance? Norman Cousins, in his opening address to the Bicentennial Symposium in Philadelphia on August 6, 1987, summarized the legacy of the Founding Fathers by ten

117

principal ideas:

1. The idea that nations can be created out of historical experience.

2. The idea that different political units or entities can be accommodated within the structure of a single government and that there is a proper and separate sphere of authority for both the individual and the collective unit of which it is a part.

3. The idea that nations within a geographic unit must unite if they don't want to fight.

4. The idea that freedom for a society, or for the individual, is possible only under law, but law must be defined not solely in terms of obligations or limitations but also in terms of rights.

5. The idea that such rights do not have to be conferred or designed by the state, but are to be regarded as biological realities, rights which come with the fact of birth, and that these rights cannot be revoked, modified, or abrogated by the state, indeed, that the state justifies its existence only as it dedicates itself to the protection and preservation of such rights;

6. The idea that the ultimate power of any nation belongs to the people who inhabit it;

7. The idea that the basic purpose of any society is to provide the conditions under which the individual can develop to his or her full talents and potentialities.

8. The idea that a nation need not topsy into existence as part of a chain of action and reaction involving upheaval, overthrow, or coup d'etat; and that it is within the reach of human intelligence to create a design for a nation built on tested principles of collective organization.

9. The idea that even good people in government can't be trusted with unchecked power; and the governmental power must be hedged with all sorts of clearly understood and structured limitations, which is to say, statutory law.

10. And, finally, the idea that moral imagination can be a genuine force in the life of the individual and is not to be scorned or disregarded in the operation of society.

A Showdown of Cosmic Proportions

I believe that we are facing a showdown of cosmic proportions between the hubris of uninhibited power and the civilizing force of reason–like the final act of an ancient Greek drama. Will it be the ultimate tragedy in which the good is destroyed by its own inadequacy, the hero's "tragic flaw"? Or will the modern furies somehow be transformed by reason, as in Aeschylus' play 2500 years ago they became "The Eumenides" or "even-tempered ones," a jury for justice, law, and order? Cord Meyer set the stage for this final act. He was a World War II Marine corps veteran who became first president of the United World Federalists. He wrote in the Epilogue to his book, *Peace or Anarchy* (1947):

"Measured against the infinite age of the earth and stars, the span of human existence is brief indeed. Yet in the comparatively few years that man has inhabited the planet, he has achieved great and wonderful things. From the caves where he once lived in savage ignorance, he has won his way to nearly complete control over his natural environment. Now he has only himself to fear. He can use his new-found power to destroy himself and all that has been built and thought through the laborious centuries, or he can find a more generous existence on this earth than ever before was possible. This is the decision which we, as the living representatives of the race, must take in our time.

"If war comes, it will not be because it was inevitable but because too many believed it to be inevitable. Let us remember that we are endowed with reason and imagination, that we are capable through intelligent, courageous action of influencing our destiny." (Cord Meyer, 233)

Those who claim the legacy of the Founding Fathers are cast in this final act. "We" may seem to be very few, and "they" seem to be many and powerful. Whether we are cast in the role of actor, or speaker with lines to say, or in the role of members of the chorus which, as in a Greek play, listens and interprets, admonishes and supports–every part is vital. There are no "bit roles." For, as Eisenhower said, "The world no longer has a choice between force and law. If civilization is to survive, it must choose the rule of law."

BIBLIOGRAPHY

Bowen, Catherine Drinker, *Miracle at Philadelphia*. Boston: Little Brown and Co., 1986.

Cousins, Norman, *"What Philadelphia 1787 Has to Say to the World of 1987."* Opening address at the International Bicentennial Symposium on Strengthening the United Nations, Philadelphia, August 6, 1987.

The Defense Monitor published by the Center for Defense Information, Washington, DC 1986 (Vol. XV, No. 3) and 1987 (Vol. XVI, No. 4)

Meyer, Cord, *Peace or Anarchy*. Boston: Little Brown and Co., 1947.

Nash, Vernon, *The World Must be Governed*. New York: Harper, 1949.

Reves, Emery, *The Anatomy of Peace*. New York: Harper, 1949.

Streit, Clarence, *Union Now*. New York: Harper, 1939.

Van Doren, Carl, *The Great Rehearsal*. New York: The Viking Press, 1948.

Waterlow, Charlotte, *Federal Constitutions for a Divided World*. London: Assn. of World Federalists, 1987.

The World Federalist Bicentennial Reader, compiled by Barbara Walker. Washington, D.C.: World Federalist Association, 1987

A CONSTITUTION FOR THE WORLD?

A logical sequence to the "Rehearsal" was this development of the idea of constitutional government from Plato to the current global situation. Four proposed constitutions for the world are compared and diagrammed. As to the prospects for any of them coming into use, or of the convening of a world constitutional convention, three paths are examined: reform of the United Nations, global statesmanship, and initiative of the people. A sign that the time might be ripe was a vote of the WGO Coalition in October to encourage its membership of two dozen organizations to promote the idea.

Plato was not noted for being a patron of the arts. He thought music and poetry, by appealing to the senses, would corrupt the youth and weaken the state. One exception, however, was the "painting of constitutions" which he considered the highest form of art, worthy only of philosophers, who of course should be kings. In describing their art, he wrote: After making a "clean surface...they will proceed to trace an outline of the constitution...and when they are filling in the work, as I conceive, they will often turn their eyes upwards and downwards: I mean that they will first look at absolute justice and beauty and temperance, and again at the human copy; and will mingle and temper the various elements of life into the image of a man; and this they will conceive according to that other image, which, when existing among men, Homer calls the form and likeness of God...And one feature they will erase and another they will put in, until they have made the ways of men, as far as possible, the ways of God." (*The Republic*, Book VI)[1]

The idea of government by means of a contract between the ruler and the ruled is a unique contribution of western culture. It can be

---

* This paper was presented to the Outlook Club of Berkeley, CA, January 4, 1990.

** To help the reader, some material in this article is repeated from the previous one, Our Constitutional Convention: Rehearsal for World Federation.

[1] Plato, *The Republic*, Book VI, in *Five Great Dialogues*. New York: D. Van Nostrand Company, Inc. 1942. pp. 385-387

traced as far back as the Book of Genesis where God made a "covenant" with Noah that "the waters shall no more become a flood to destroy all flesh" which was duly signed: "And the (rain)bow shall be in the cloud; and I will look upon it, that I may remember the everlasting covenant between God and every living creature of all flesh that is upon the earth." (Genesis 9: 15&16) God's side of the contract has been honored so far, at least in the literal sense. (The "Heavenly Landlord" has not yet issued an eviction notice.) Noah's side remained somewhat ambiguous until the Ten Commandments were "dictated" to Moses, the Law-giver. Although honored too often in the breach, they continue to be a foundation of western law, spelled out in writing, for governance of the human community. As it was in later times, the Covenant of the Hebrews may be seen to be more of an attempt to bring the Ruler under control than the ruled!

Twenty-four centuries later the Magna Carta extorted from King John in 1215 a.d. the first conditions of English liberty. Among its thirty-seven clauses directed principally against abuses of power by the Crown, was the guarantee that no subject should be kept in prison without trial and judgment by his peers. Nearly five centuries later further rights and privileges of the people were spelled out in the Bill of Rights of 1688 as conditions under which William of Orange was allowed to occupy the British throne. The next century was to see the flowering of the idea of government under "a known and written law" both in philosophy and in practice.

John Locke (1632-1705), whose philosophy was largely incorporated in the Bill of 1688, believed that "The great and chief end of men uniting into commonwealths, and putting themselves under governments, is the preservation of property; to which in the state of nature there are many things wanting." Among these things, he said, were "an established, settled, known law," "a known and indifferent judge" and "power to back and support the sentence when right, and to give it due execution" — in other words, a constitution, a judiciary and an executive. To these he added a "supreme" legislative power elected by the people, but bound, itself, by the standing laws and known authorized judges. Locke's influence on the American Constitution is evident. [2]

---

2. John Locke, *Of Civil Governemnt, Two Treatises*, in *Preface to Philosophy*, Hoople, Piper & Tolley, Editors. New York: The Macmillan Company, 1946. pp. 233-242

Jean Jacques Rousseau (1712-1778) spelled out in more radical terms the role of the social contract in creating equality and liberty under the law. To this Frenchman it was the accumulation of property that made men unequal and caused most of the evils of civilization such as greed, corruption and exploitation. Equality, which is a "given" in nature, is restored by a social contract in which each person gives up the same rights in return for his participation in community decision-making. Thus all people become — on an equal basis — both "citizens, as participating in the sovereign power, and subjects, as subjected to the laws of the state." As he says, "the social compact establishes among the citizens such an equality that they all pledge themselves under the same conditions and ought to enjoy the same rights." and "So long as the subjects submit only to such conventions (of the social contract), they obey no one, but simply their own will;" Thus Rousseau defines both equality and liberty under the law, ideas which were reflected in the rousing slogans of the French Revolution.[3]

Immanuel Kant (1742-1804) was the first actually to outline a charter of articles for world peace. In his *Perpetual Peace*, published in 1795, he listed these conditions as:

I. "No treaty of peace shall be esteemed valid, on which is tacitly reserved matter for future war.

II. "Any state, of whatever extent, shall never pass under the dominion of another state, whether by inheritance, exchange, purchase, or donation."

III. "Standing armies shall in time be totally abolished."

IV. "National debts shall not be contracted with a view of maintaining the interests of the state abroad."

V. "No state shall by force interfere with either the constitution or government of another state."

VI. "A state shall not during war, admit of hostilities of a nature that would render reciprocal confidence in peace impossible: such as employing assassins, prisoners, violation of capitulations, secret instigation to rebellion, etc."

Kant goes on to elaborate three "definitive articles for a perpetual peace" for, he says, a state of nature is not a state of peace, but requires legislation to be established. The **first article is:** "The Civil con-

---

[3] Jean Jaques Rousseau, *Social Contract*, 1762. in ibid, pp.242-55

stitution of every state ought to be republican." By this he means based on a social compact which establishes liberty and equality of each "man" under a common legislation which they shared in creating. According to this form, he thought, the assent of every citizen would be required to declare war, which would be highly unlikely, as they would be voting against their interests as people who bear the burdens of war, whereas without such a constitution, "a declaration of war is a most easy matter to resolve upon, as it does not require of the chief...the least sacrifice of his pleasures..." The **second definitive article is:** "The public ought to be founded upon a federation of free states." By this he means that such constitutional governments as are based on social contracts should unite in a similar contract with each other, in which each renounces the right to make war while retaining the internal liberties guaranteed by its own constitution. (This is a statement of the "minimalist" position on world federation, which will be illustrated later in this paper.) In Kant's own words, "At the tribunal of reason there is but one means of extricating states from this turbulent situation in which they are constantly menaced by war; namely, to renounce, like individuals, the anarchic liberty of savages, in order to submit themselves to coercive laws, and thus to form a society of nations which would insensibly embrace all the nations of the earth." *The* **third definitive article is:** "The cosmopolitical right shall be limited to conditions of universal hospitality." Hospitality here signifies solely the right of a citizen of one state not to be treated as an enemy by another, including the right to be admitted to that state without hostility, "so long as he does not offend any one." (This is perhaps an early statement of the idea of world citizenship, as he calls it "a right founded on that of the common possession of the surface of the earth...and because originally one has not a greater right to a country than another." Kant was well aware of "how great a distance from this perfection are the civilized nations, and especially the commercial nations of Europe," he said, but added that it is a state of perfection "to which one cannot hope to continually advance, except by means here indicated." [4]

The United States of America embodied in its Constitution of 1789

---

[4] Immanuel Kant, *Perpetual Peace,* in ibid, pp295-299

many of these intellectual currents of thought. It was the first practical constitution for the operation of a federal government. The process by which it was created was presented in a previous paper to the Outlook Club (March 17, 1988). It was said to be a "miracle" that such a Constitution was achieved at all, but it was to become the longest living federal constitution in the world, at least to date. We are reminded that, like Kant, some of the founding fathers saw the implications of their work for the whole world, thought of the Constitution as a model for the whole human race, and of themselves as world citizens. George Washington called himself "a citizen of the great republic of humanity at large". Gouverneur Morris of Pennsylvania said he came to the Convention... "in some degree as a representative of the whole human race; for the whole human race will be affected by the proceedings of this convention." Benjamin Franklin wrote, in 1788, "God grant, that not only the love of liberty, but a thorough knowledge of the Rights of Man, may pervade all the nations of the earth, so that a philsopher may set his foot anywhere on its surface, and say, 'This is my country.'"

Two centuries later, there are over one hundred countries that now have a social contract or constitution as a basis of government. These may differ somewhat in form and application, but many of them are patterned after the U.S. Constitution, and at least seventeen are federal in structure. The latter are listed in the World Federalist Reader roughly in the chronological order of their first federal constitutions:

Argentina (1816,1829,1853,1880)
Mexico (1814,1821,1857,1917)
Brazil (1822,1891)
Venezuela (1830,1864)
Switzerland (1848)
Germany (1866,1871,1919,1949)
Canada (1867)
Austria-Hungary (1867)
Australia (1901)
Yugoslavia (1918,1953)
Austria (1920,1953)
Czechoslovakia (1920, 1948, 1960)
USSR (1922, 1936, 1977)
India (1949)
Pakistan (1956, 1962)
Malaya (1957) and Malaysia (1963)
Nigeria (1960)

In addition, some strictly unitary states have had, or been given recently some federalist features: Union of South Africa (1910), Italy (1948), Burma (1948), China (1949), Ethiopia and Eritrea (1952), Tanzania (1964), Belgium (1980) and Spain (1982). There are also "nascent federations" in regional associations of states like the Organization of American States (1948), the Non-Aligned Movement (1961), and the Organization of Afican Unity (1963). [5]

Government by contract or constitution has become, in the last two hundred years, a familiar and generally accepted form of organization for the nations of the world. However, it has still to be applied in practice to a world community of nations, although models have emerged that are suggestive of the shape that community might someday take. Let us turn at this point to some of the modern "painters of constitutions" who have — individually or in groups — designed some of the blue prints for a governed world. I have chosen four among the world constitutions to describe because they are different in origin, have some unique characteristics, and because I am somewhat familiar with them. They are: *A Constitution for the World,* first published in 1948 in *Common Cause by* the Committee to Frame a World Constitution at the Santa Barbara Center for the Study of Democractic Institutions; *World Constitution: Study on the Legal Framework of a World Constitution* by Thomas Breitner, first appearing in the U.S. *Daily Californian* on May 10, 1966, written by a staff member of the University; *The World Federation Constitution (Draft)* by a Research Committee of distinguished Japanese (1980); and *A Constitution for the Federation of Earth,* the collective work of more than one hundred individuals from twenty-five countries, first presented for "ratification" in 1977 by the World Constitution and Parliament Association.

The first and oldest is perhaps the best known. *A Constitution for the World* [6] was created by a committee of prominent Americans, including Robert Hutchins, President, G.A. Borgese, Secretary and Mortimer Adler, all from the University of Chicago, and Stringfellow Barr and other notables from U.S. universities. Dedicated to Ma-

---

[5]. Joseph Baratta, "The Spirit of Federalism: From Philadelphia in 1787 to the World in 1987", in *World Federalist Bicentennial Reader,* published by World Federalist Association, Washington, D.C., 1987. pp. 132-133

[6] *A Constitution for the World,* published in book form at the Center for the Study of Democratic Institutions, Santa Barbara, CA 1965

hatma Gandhi, the "Precursor" and model of "whoever will deserve to be World President," the preliminary draft came out shortly after Gandhi's death. Later published in book form in 1965 by the Center for the Study of Democractic Institutions, the *Constitution* "is founded on the Rights of Man... (and) "in the Duty of everyone everywhere, whether a citizen sharing in the responsibilities and provileges of World Government or a ward and pupil of the World Commonwealth". The rights include just four paragraphs: on release from poverty; servitude and exploitation of labor; on freedom of assembly and association; on protection against subjugation and tyrannical rule, with safeguards for minorities; and on "inalienable claims to life, liberty, and the dignity of the human person." In addition, the four elements of life — earth, water, air, energy — are declared "the common property of the human race. The management and use of such portions thereof as are vested in or assigned to particular ownership, private or corporate or national or regional, of definite or indefinite tenure, of individualist or collectivist economy, shall be subordinated in each and all cases to the interest of the common good." Chart 1 (opposite this page) diagrams the structure of the proposed government.

Note that ultimate "sovereignty" lies in The People of the World — the basic principle of democracy. Note too that there is no direct representation of nations as such. This is the only constitution of the four which is not a federation of states. The "Federal Convention," is elected by the people on the basis of population (one delegate for each million people) who vote as individuals, not as members of national or other entities. This contrasts sharply with the current United Nations, in which people are not represented — only nations, many of which do not even represent *indirectly* the people of their countries. The "Federal Convention" subdivides itself — not into nations, but into 9 regions, such as the continent of Europe, Eurasia, Asia Major, Africa, etc. These are called Electoral Colleges, and they elect the President and World Council of ninety-nine members. The council is the legislative body, the President the administrative body, each with a check on the other's power, much like that in the USA. Together they appoint the Justices of the Grand Tribunal, with the President serving as Chief Justice and the Chairman of the Council as Vice-

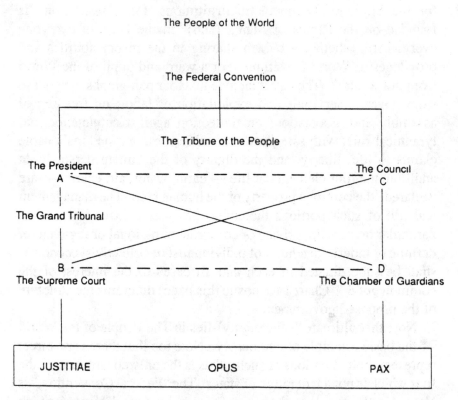

The People of the World

The Federal Convention

The Tribune of the People

The President
A

The Council
C

The Grand Tribunal

B

D

The Supreme Court

The Chamber of Guardians

JUSTITIAE   OPUS   PAX

Dotted Line AC symbolizes intervention of Council in tenure of the President's Cabinet and Acting Presidency of the Chairman of the Council during vacancies in the Presidency.

Diagonal AD symbolizes Chairmanship of the President in the Chamber of Guardians.

Diagonal CB symbolizes Council's veto power on appointments to the Judiciary and membership of the Chairman of the Council in the Tribunal and Supreme Court.

Dotted Line BD symbolizes intervention of the Judiciary in elections to the Chamber of Guardians.

CHART 1

128

Chairman. The Justices are divided into five Benches dealing with different issues: constitutional, inter-government, between citizens and government agencies, etc. The Supreme Court is made up of a representative of each Bench plus the Chief Justice and Vice Chairman — seven members. Its function is to assign cases to the different Benches and review the decisions made by them. Control and use of the armed forces is exclusively in the hands of a six-member Chamber of Guardians under the chairmanship of the President in his capacity as Protector of the Peace. The Guardians are elected jointly by the Council and Grand Tribunal for terms of three years. The government will choose a site for a "Federal" Capital, an official language for government purposes, and an official unit of currency, a system of measurements and a "federal" calendar. Finally, the World Republic is prohibited from making any law that discriminates against a race, nation, sex or creed; that bars any state from equal access to raw materials; that permits arbitrary seizure or search, abridges freedom of speech, etc. Capital punishment is prohibited, and certain social services are guaranteed by grants or loans from government, such as old age pensions, insurance against sickness or accident, maternity and infancy care and equal access to education. In summary, we could say that this Constitution for the World is not federalist in the usual sense, but more like a democratic republic, with built-in balance of powers and a broad or "maximalist" application to social and economic areas.

The second constitution is entirely different. First of all, it was essentially the work of a single person, a laboratory technician in biophysics. Having lost his family in the Holocaust, he escaped from a labor camp at the age of eighteen and made his way from Hungary to France, where he joined the U.S. Army. He was determined to do something that would prevent the occurrence of such massive atrocities in the future. His work is called *World Constitution: Study on the Legal Framework of a World Federation,* [7] first printed in Berkeley in 1963, and appearing three years later in the campus Daily Californian in three parts. The first part, titled "Evolution Towards a Worldwide Commonwealth of Man," is an "outgrowth of a deeply felt, solemn

[7] Thomas Breitner, *World Constitution: Study on the Legal Framework of a World Federation.* Berkeley, CA 1963

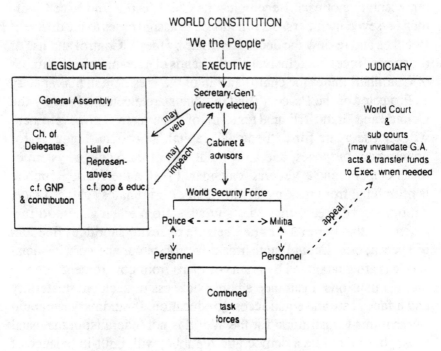

WORLD CONSTITUTION
"We the People"

| LEGISLATURE | EXECUTIVE | JUDICIARY |

General Assembly

Secretary-Gen'l.
(directly elected)

World Court
&
sub courts
(may invalidate G.A.
acts & transfer funds
to Exec. when needed

| Ch. of Delegates | Hall of Represen-tatives |
| c.f. GNP & contribution | c.f. pop & educ. |

may veto

may impeach

Cabinet & advisors

World Security Force

Police <- - - - - - - -> Militia

appeal

Personnel   Personnel

Combined task forces

Safeguards for the World Security Force:
Two co-equal bodies--may court-martial each other's officers
Personnel's oath to obey Constitution, not individuals
If disobey orders, must prove them unconstitutional
If court martialled, may appeal to civil courts
Required to use minimum force necessary
Commanders may be impeached by Legislature
Civilians may take complaints of abuse to courts

CHART 2

concern and conviction that now, during the closing decades of the twentieth century, mankind itself faces... a uniquely fateful... evolutionary crisis" due to the proliferation of nuclear weapons in the "absence of proper, world-encompassing institutional safeguards."

In the second part titled "Outlines of a World Constitution," Mr. Breitner cites the U.S. experience of successful change from a confederacy to federal government as precedent for the necessary transition to a democractic world federation. On a world scale for a long time to come, he said, "only indirect devices of democracy will be practical" due to cultural and ethnic diversity. Therefore, nations are retained as the building blocks of the world government, being guaranteed certain sovereignties over their internal affairs while giving up the right to wage aggressive war or manufacture nuclear explosives. A bicameral legislature is envisioned much like that in the U.S., but with two chambers representing nations, one according to population and educational levels, and the other chamber weighted according to "such basic social parameters as economic productivity." Together they form the General Assembly or Legislative body. The Executive body, or Secretary General is elected by a majority vote of the citizenry of all the member countries and must take an oath "to faithfully serve all mankind, uphold the laws.. of the World Federation... and preserve, protect and defend the Constitution..." Among other duties, he is in charge of the World Security Force.

This last I find the most interesting feature of Mr. Breitner's Constitution because of the intricate check-and-balance system within the Security Force. It is to be composed of two co-equal bodies, a world police and world miltia, each with the authority to check on abuses of power by officers of the other body. Service personnel have the right, even duty, to disobey the orders of superiors when such orders are in violation of the Constitution. They also have the right of appeal to the higher civilian courts of the World Judiciary in cases of court-martial. Further guarding against abuses by both forces, members are recruited from all the nations within the Federation and must be of high moral and intellectual calibre. Generals should be from the smaller countries preferably, for political reasons, and finally, the Security Force itself operates under the authority of a civilian cabinet officer.

131

In short, Mr. Breitner's democratic world federation is patterned generally on the U.S. model with a tripartite system of Executive, Judiciary and a bicameral Legislature, with the addition of weighted factors of population and socio-economic conditions. He puts special attention to a check-and-balance system in the World Security Force to guard against a run-away military, and has, in addition, an extensive Bill of Rights (mostly legal), and an imaginative section on Space Law.

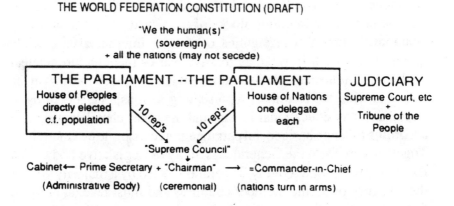

THE WORLD FEDERATION CONSTITUTION (DRAFT)

"We the human(s)"
(sovereign)
+ all the nations (may not secede)

THE PARLIAMENT --THE PARLIAMENT   JUDICIARY

House of Peoples   House of Nations   Supreme Court, etc
directly elected   one delegate   +
c.f. population   each   Tribune of the People

10 rep's   10 rep's

"Supreme Council"

Cabinet ← Prime Secretary + "Chairman" ⟶ =Commander-in-Chief

(Administrative Body)   (ceremonial)   (nations turn in arms)

CHART 3

The third constitution is a draft by a Research Committee of Japanese Federalists which was presented to the 18th World Congress of World Federalists in Tokyo in July, 1980.[1] It is even more traditional, in the sense that it follows more closely the U.S. Constitution and the United Nations Charter. Although it opens with "We the human(s) of the world declare the sovereignty rests with the human(s) to save eternally the human(s) from the scourge of war...", Article 1 in Chapter I says "The World Federation shall consist of all the nations." Two houses make up the Parliament: the House of Nations with one delegate from each of the Affiliated Nations, and a House of

---

[1] *The World Federation Constitution (Draft)* by the Research Committee on Drafting of the World Federation Constitution, Japan. 1980

Peoples with members elected directly by the people of all the Affiliated Nations in proportion to population. These bodies elect ten each of their members to a "Supreme Council" with a ceremonial "Chairman" and an administrative "Prime Secretary" who presides over the Cabinet, which is the administrative body of the government. The judiciary body consists of the traditional Supreme Court and its subsidiary courts. A police force would be made up of candidates from the Affiliated Nations with the Chairman of the Council as Commander-in-Chief. Armaments of the nations would be turned over to the World Police Force. A Tribune of the People (or Ombudsman) would be established to protect the people from any illicit actions of the government., Finally, the Constitution would come into force upon the ratification by two-thirds of the Affiliated Nations. In summary, this is the simplest and most easily recognized of the four constitutions — mainly structural, with minimum reference to human rights. Only the rights to social security and education are mentioned. This is perhaps compensated for by the provision of a directly elected House of Peoples — an idea currently being proposed to the United Nations, which will be presented later.

In sharp contrast to this — in fact, to all the other three constitutions — is the fourth, *A Constitution for the Federation of Earth.* [9] It is the work of over one hundred individuals from twenty-five countries during a period of nineteen years before June, 1977. Then it was signed and adopted by participants in a World Constituent Assembly in Innsbrook, Austria. By far the most comprehensive of the constitutions, it has become the basis of a grass-roots effort to create a provisional world government. The prospects for this as well as other efforts will be considered in the last section of this paper. Here we will describe the content of the Constitution itself:

From the Preamble and Article I it is clear that the broad functions of the world goverment would extend beyond the abolition of war to ensuring human rights, economic and social justice and protection of the environment — in other words, this is a maximalist rather than minimalist plan. As shown in the diagram, the ultimate sovereignty lies with the people, who are represented in an elected House of

---

[9.] A *Constitution for the Federation of Earth*, published by the World Constitution and Parliament Association, Lakewood, Colorado, 1977

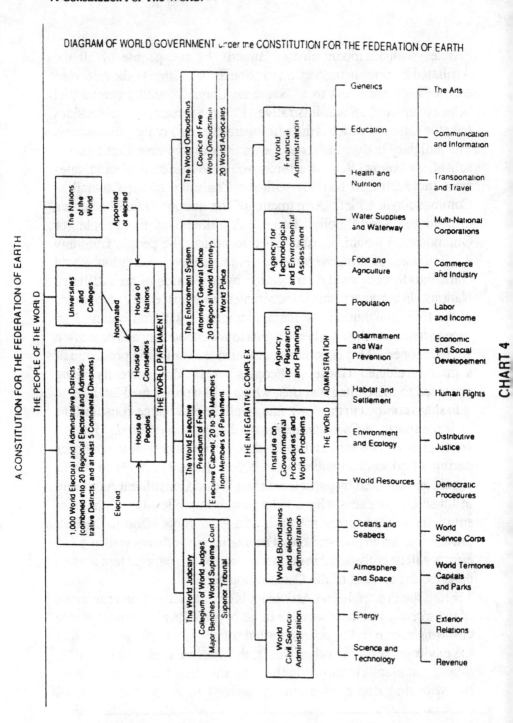

DIAGRAM OF WORLD GOVERNMENT under the CONSTITUTION FOR THE FEDERATION OF EARTH

CHART 4

Peoples, while nations are also represented by delegates either appointed or elected to a House of Nations. To these two are added a House of Counsellors or wise men and women nominated at large by teachers and students from the universities and colleges. With this innovation, the Parliament is made up of three houses, the Counsellors serving as advisors and mediators to the other two houses.

Some notable features of this constitution are: that the Executive may not veto, transcend or contradict decisions of the Parliament or Judiciary bodies (Article VI, Section F); a system of world ombudsmen is established in twenty regional offices in addition to the primary seat of the World Government (Article XI, Section B 5); the Bill of Rights includes, along with all the usual items, freedom to profess no religion as well as any religion, prohibition against private armies, the right to free public assistance in family planning (Article XII) and under Article XIII: free and adequate public health services, encouragement for cultural diversity and decentralized administration, peaceful self-determination for minorities, freedom of change of residence to anywhere on earth, and prohibition against the death penalty. Probably the most controvertial aspect of the Constitution is its non-military enforcement system (Article X, Sections A and D), which declares that the World Government "shall neither keep nor use weapons of mass destruction: and that its agents "shall be equipped only with such weapons as are appropriate for the apprehension of the individuals responsible for violation." This applies to external enemies as well as internal, the argument being that no weapons of mass destruction could prevail in a nuclear world, and that security lies in avoiding rather than preparing for a military show-down. (A abasic tenet of federalism is, of course, the right of the federal government to arrest individual violators of the federal laws within affiliated states, rather than waging war against the whole state.) To sum up, this constitution provides for a democratic, federal government in maximalist terms, with responsibilities for social and economic as well as political justice and environmental sustainability. It is also a non-military government.

In the final section of this paper, I would like to consider the question which, I am sure, is already on all of your minds, namely, what are the prospects of any of these constitutions coming into use

–or better yet, of a constitutional convention being called to form, out of these and other such works a Constitution for the World?

It is a truism to say that the world is facing a crisis. Governments are crumbling under the impact of an explosion of people power in Eastern Europe–"The End of History" says Francis Fukuyama, in a final victory of western-style democracy. Unfortunately, this latter is too often interpreted as mere economic freedom of enterprise rather than political and legal freedom under constitutional law, on which western-style democracy is based. Corruption of the latter by the so-called "free market" is evident in the greed by which traffic in drugs and weapons destroys people; the growing gap between rich and poor destroys equality of economic opportunity (along with corporate takeovers, bank failures, under-funded education, housing and medical care); and a run-away secret service destroys political liberty and equality under the law–surely not an acceptable "end to history"! Better to call an end to economic and political ideology and a beginning to practical problem-solving on a global scale. The business of an interdependent world cannot be managed on a for-profit basis while the environment deteriorates and the population continues to explode. Nor can it be administered for the common good and future generations by one hundred-sixty independent states. Sheer pragmatism demands a clear statement of the common goals of the human race and adjustment of means toward those goals. That, after all, is what a constitution is about. Will the people's revolt against the anachronisms of ideology and nationalism lead, at the end of this century, to anarchy — or to a new, more civilized world order with global institutions adequate to deal rationally with global problems? That is the question.

In Chinese, the term for "crisis" contains two characters; one for "danger" and one for "opportunity." Along with many apparent dangers in the present crisis, there are opportunities opening that could not have been anticipated two years ago: for example, the remarkable phenomenon of Mikhail Gorbachev who, on December 7, 1988 said to the United Nations,[10]"Our ideal is a world community of states which are based on the rule of law and which subordinate their

---

[10] Reprinted in "News and Views from the USSR", by the Consulate General, USSR in San Francisco p. 15

foreign policies to law;" the evolution of Europe toward just such a community, with the suggestion even of a merger of the NATO and Warsaw Treaty Organizations;[11] and the call by one hundred-two Non Aligned Nations for a Decade of International Law.[12]

In this next decade a constitution for the world could be brought about by (1) reform of the U.N.; (2) global statesmanship; or (3) initiative of the people. The **first way**, United Nations reform, has been the preferred method by most Federalists up to now. There are good reasons. The U.N. Charter is a noble document, already established and operating successfully in many specialized areas where it is authorized to act, including the area of peacekeeping. It has also served as a global forum for the nations' delegates to discuss the issues among themselves and to let off steam. Two basic shortcomings of the Charter would have to be addressed in order to transform the U.N. into a democratic federation: one being that there is no provision for participation by the people except through their national embassies (appointed by their heads of state). The other shortcoming is, of course, the voting procedure by which every state has an equal vote in the General Assembly regardless of size, experience, or financial contribution. This gives the five biggest nations the need to have a veto in the Security Council over issues involving money or military enforcement. The Charter is, in fact, based on "the sovereign equality of all its Members" (Chapter I Article 2), which is the structural flaw of a confederacy. The only way to change the Charter requires a two-thirds majority of the General Assembly and all five of the members that have a veto. The likelihood of "sovereign" nations, large or small, cutting off their own power by such a procedure has been likened to a person's taking out his own appendix–in the view of skeptics about this path to world government.

Another possibility is that the change could come about through the leadship of some global statesmen who, by their understanding and their position of power, could initiate a world constitutional convention. There have been many leaders of such stature recently who have shown an undersatnding of the need for world government.

---

11. See John Mueller, "European Solution: Combine NATO, Warsaw Pact" in the *San Francisco Chronicle*, Briefing Section, December 6, 1989

12. See United Nations General Assembly publication A/44/191, 27 July 1989, "United Nations Decade of International Law" 89-18339 1146j (E)

Quotations could be given from Einstein, Truman, Nehru, Churchill, MacArthur, Eisenhower, Kennedy, Golda Meir, U Thant, Willy Brandt, Pope John Paul II, and many others. None have come as close to acting on it, however, as Mikhail Gorbachev and George Bush. The rapproachment of these two may turn out to be what is known in world government circles as "the shotgun wedding approach." Each, looking down the barrel of a shotgun (economic disaster, nuclear war, etc.), decides it's better, after all, to get married. Whether this wedding will make a happy marriage or a bitter divorce remains to be seen, but all the couple's relations have good reasons to wish them well!

The third possibility is a grass-roots initiative by the people. Organized protest against government policies has been on the rise for decades in the West, but nobody anticipated the explosion of anti-government demonstrations in the East in recent years. Together, these represent a rising tide of resentment by the people over corruption, bureaucracy and state-centered priorities that fail to meet real human needs. This is largely due to the extravagance of the arms race on both sides, a by-product of the global anarchy among so-called "sovereign" states in an interdependent world. The democracy movements in the East have been the more forceful and effective in changing their governments–perhaps due to the sudden release of pent-up resentment, but that resentment has long been shared by protesters in the West against nuclear war, poverty, and environmental abuse. The "critical mass" now approaching creates a "crisis" replete with both "danger" and "opportunity"–danger that the people who find themselves, perhaps inadvertently, in positions of power are unable to manage their country's problems, and are overthrown by force, setting things back to the beginning again –and "opportunity" for a global restructuring toward a democractic world federation with civilized ways of settling disputes and adequate machinery to solve global problems. Chances for the latter may seem remote, but they are not impossible in the current flux of history. Some up-coming events at least point in the right direction. One is the convening in October of representatives of a worldwide network of organizations promoting a second "Peoples" house in the United Nations. This movement has grown to incorporate over one hundred non-government organizations (NGO's) and a dozen different proposals, which will be brought together in an attempt to achieve a common effort. Another is a World Constituent Assembly called for by the World Constitution and Parliament Association, promoter of *A Constitution for the Federation of Earth* to review the Constitution, debate and adopt amendments and "To launch a final and rapid global campaign for ratification of the amended Earth Constitution by the people and governments of Earth." (Call to a World Constituent Assembly) It may be a surprise that governments, especially in Asia and the Third World, are beginning to show some interest in both of these projects.

In conclusion, while the "painter of constitutions" may fall short of Plato's ideal of making "the ways of men, as far as possible, the ways of God", they have at least designed ways of avoiding the most gruesome alternatives. As long as the original covenant that Noah made with the "Heavenly Landlord" remains in force, His rainbow is still in the sky and we earthly tenants are not evicted from this planet, there is at least the possibility of "A Constitution for the World." In view of the rate at which events are now moving, I would even put a small amount of money on it being initiated by the year 2000.

SOME OTHER SOURCES FOR A WORLD CONSTITUTION

1. *Charter of the United Nations and Statute of the International Court of Justice* available from the Office of Information, United Nations, New York
2. Shigetsugu Nakao, *A Tentative Plan for the Establishment of a World Federation*, Garden Grove, CA: World Federation Research Institute, 1975
3. Clark, Grenville and Louis Sohn, *World Peace Through World Law*, Cambridge, MA, Harvard University Press, 1958, 1960, 1962
4. Emery Reves, *The Anatomy of Peace*. New York: Harper & Brothers, 1945; Viking, 1963
5. "Draft of a World Constitution" in *Mundialist Summa*, vol I, *One World of Reason*. Paris, France: Club Humaniste, 1977. pp. 75-78
6. Clarence Streit, *Union Now: A Proposal for an Atlantic Federal Union of the Free*. New York: Harper & Brothers, 1939
7. Warren Wagar, *The City of Man*. Boston: Houghton-Mifflin, 1963

Logo of the World Federalist Association and World Federalist-USA until 1989

ROOTS OF A WORLD DEMOCRACY

In this year when movements for "democracy" and "freedom" encircle the earth, and when talk of a "a new world order" comes out of the crisis in the Middle East, it behooves us to examine the meaning of these powerful ideas before they are extrapolated to a global institution, such as a peoples' house in the United Nations. Although the first limited application of the idea of democracy was in Greece at the time of Pericles about 450 B.C., the next generation of Greek philosophers held the idea in contempt. Plato and Aristotle considered it about the worst form of government next to tyranny: "...a charming form of government, full of variety and disorder, and dispensing a sort of equality to equals and unequals alike." (Plato's *Republic:* Book VIII) Even as late as the nineteenth century, Frederich Nietzche considered it a perversion of the natural order of excellence, that is, of the "noble" over the "vulgar."

It was philosophers of the "Age of Reason" (17th-19th centuries) that proclaimed the idea in England (John Locke) and France (Rousseau) that governments are created to serve the people, not visa versa. Locke, in opposition to the "divine right of kings," insisted on "an established, settled, known law" to which even kings were subject, "a known and indifferent judge" with "power to back and support the sentence when right" and a "supreme" legislative power elected by the people, but bound *itself* by the standing laws and authorized judges –in other words, a constitution, a judiciary, and a legislative body to represent the people. Jean Jacques Rousseau elaborated the idea in his *Social Contract* (1762). The people, in order to regain "freedom" and "equality," (which are givens in nature) must establish a compact in society between the rulers and the ruled in which members freely determine the form of government and the laws

---

* This was an opening address given at the first international Conference on a more Democractic United Nations (CAMDUN-I) in New York, October 13, 1990.

which they agree to obey. The "freedom" of citizens, unlike freedom in nature (or anarchy) is the right to help create their form of government and the laws by which they abide. Since each person gives up the same "natural rights" in return for participation in community decision-making, all people are –on an equal basis –both citizens and subjects of the state. As Rousseau said, "So long as the subjects submit only to such conventions (as the *Social Contract*), they obey no one, but simply their own will." Thus Rousseau deliniated the ideas of "freedom" and "equality" *under the law* which have become basic tenets of democracy.

These ideas were institutionalized in the Constitution of the United States in 1789, the first practical constitution for the operation of a democractic federation of states. The ultimate "sovereignty" of the people lies in the right to vote and participate in government; "freedom" and "equality" are embedded in the Bill of Rights. The House of Representatives (at that time called the "First House") represents the people according to population, and the Senate the states, large and small on an equal basis (as now in the United Nations).

It is evident from the statements by some of the Founding Fathers that they thought of their constitution as a model for the rest of the world. For example, George Washington had come to think of himself, in his own words, "a citizen of the great republic of humanity at large." Gouverneur Morris of Pennsylvania came to the convention in his words, "in some degree as a representative of the whole human race; for the whole human race will be affected by the proceedings of this Convention." Benjamin Franklin wrote to a friend in Paris in 1787, "I do not see why you might not in Europe ... (form) "One Grand Republick of all the different States and Kingdoms, by means of a like Convention," and a year later, "God grant, that not only the love of liberty, but a thorough knowledge of the Rights of Man, may pervade all the Nations of the Earth, so that a Philosopher may set his Foot anywhere on its Surface, and say, 'This is my Country.'"

Indeed now, two centuries later, over one hundred countries have a social contract or constitution as their basis of government, though not all are democratic in form or practice. The contract has become a familiar way of organization for the nations of the world, but still remains to be applied to a world community. The Charter of the United Nations is, as its name implies, a contract among the nations, not between the people and the nations (in spite of the opening words, "We the peoples of the United Nations"). It remains to be established that people, rather than nations, are ultimately "sovereign" if there is to be a world democracy. A Peoples' House –or something like it – could be a step in that direction *if* the vision is clear and the roots are deep.

There is one aspect of the vision of democracy that needs to be clarified. That is the connection between political and economic "democracy." It is risky, I think, to identify democracy with market economy or so-called "free enterprise." It seems as though the three branches of the tree proclaimed by the French revolution: "liberty, equality and fraternity," were separated at the roots, and "liberty" developed westward at the expense of equality and fraternity, while equality and fraternity developed eastward at the expense of liberty. How can they be re-united in a political-economic system that will really foster the growth of human potential? That, after all, is the virtue of democracy — not to be an end in itself, but a means (and perhaps the best political one so far created) of nurturing the human spirit by providing it with freedom of choice and responsibility. This is needed in economic as well as political arenas, and the ideal combination is still to be made clear, at least to me. I am an American, but I do not hold America to be a model of economic equality, fraternity or even justice. Our "unalienable Rights (to) life, liberty and pursuit of Happiness" are too often interpreted to mean "life, liberty and pursuit of Property." Pursuit of property is not conducive to the growth of human potential, in my opinion, nor to a sustainable environment, or a democratic body politic. More humane, it seems to me is the idea of "From each according to his ability; to each according to his need." What formula or formulae could unite the best of East and West? I do not know the answer. Perhaps it would be a good problem for some future World Citizens Assembly? What would be an economy of the people, by the people, *for the people?*

Finally, what about the crisis in the Middle East –its danger and

143

its opportunity *for us?* Never have we seen such a convergence of purpose among nations, East, West, North and South, whether it is due to their looking down the barrel of a gun or barrel of oil. At this moment in history an emergency assembly of world powers is called for to deliberate and devise – not only an equitable solution to this crisis–but a better way to resolve the other seething issues in the Middle East. Most important of all, it could lay the foundations of a new kind of world order in which such problems are solved in a civilized way though the impartial courts and enforceable laws. We would do well, it seems to me, to give our support to such an enterprise. (Even an ounce of weight, according to a Chinese proverb, when exerted at the right time and place, can determine the direction of a ton of matter.) We should *insist* that the voice of the people be heard at this assembly, for every man, woman and child on earth is a hostage to the Old World Order's countdown to Armageddon.

The roots of democracy are deep and spreading fast: East, West, North and South, including among the people of the Arab world. So let us make sure that the New World Order to emerge from this crisis will *at last* replace the Law of Force with the Force of Law, will protect the rights of all people to life, liberty, economic justice and a sustainable environment; and that it will provide for the *voice* of the people to be heard and the *will* of the people to prevail over the warring nations on this Earth.

EPILOGUE:

LOOKING AHEAD

ONLY ONE EARTH

AND IT'S
IN OUR HANDS

Logo of the Association of World Citizens and World Citizens Assembly

LOOKING AHEAD
PERSPECTIVE ON THE MOVEMENTS
FOR PEACE AND A GOVERNED WORLD

*A very personal assessment
in anguish—and in hope*

The Bomb that fell on Hiroshima in 1945—has it really changed our way of thinking? Today there are the equivalent of over one million Hiroshima bombs in the combined arsenals of the nuclear powers. Do we really understand what would happen if they were used? Even if a possible nuclear disaster is averted, a *certain* disaster as terminal as nuclear war is well on the way in our environment barring a global effort on the scale of the arms race to avert it. We *know* these things, but how have they changed our way of thinking? Have we simply accepted them as the way of life? Why do we continue to put up with these monstrous threats to the *survival of our planet?* In an experiment, frogs dropped suddenly into hot water would immediately jump out, while those put into cool water which was then gradually heated, stayed until they were too weak to jump and cooked to death. Isn't there a parallel to people—even in the peace movement—who accept things like "arms control" (which means controlled increase in weapons) instead of concentrating on how to abolish the war system?

The peace movement, like the anti-slavery movement of the 19th century, has grown in size and complexity over most of this century. But it has yet to become an anti-war movement. It has been anti-draft, anti-nuclear, anti-Vietnam, etc., but has largely ignored the problem of how to abolish war—*how to get out of hot water.* Today the peace movement is reaching a critical mass in numbers, evidenced

147

by the fact that some leaders are addressing more basic issues. Some heads of state (for example, of Costa Rica, Mexico, Portugal, India and the U.S.S.R.) have said things at the U.N. like "We will abolish war by the year 2000," "create a non-violent world order," and "a world community under law." If a parallel to the anti-slavery movement can be drawn, we may be approaching the final—and most important—*political stage of the movement.* It is more critical than ever to determine where to put our energies, for we may not have a second chance.

Are we in danger of blowing it by merely protesting against what we already know to be wrong? (Way back in the 1950's a cartoon pictured "Humanity" nailed to a cross marked "Nuclear War" with the caption, "Forgive them not—for they know what they do!") Or will we just be rearranging furniture on the deck of the Titanic? What will it profit a man to escape the draft and be incinerated in a nuclear war? Or a woman to gain control over her body and be done in by toxic air, water and food? And what will it profit to freeze nuclear weapons in a world of biological and chemical warfare? What does it profit to be "adjusted" in an unjust world? It's not that we should stop doing these things, but we must now examine our priorities, especially for this critical period. Many battles can be won while the war is lost. But if the war is won, we will survive to accomplish the rest.

I used to tell my students, "If you can keep your head in times like these, you just don't understand the situation." And I admit that I, like other people, tend to keep my head by trying to forget the situation. I would rather be gardening, or swimming, or having pool parties—all busy work, I suppose, that keeps me relatively "sane." But there are moments of anguish, usually in the silence of the night, when I think about my 5-year old grandson twenty years from now, about the adorable baby animals I see on TV, about redwood trees, flowers and bird songs—all the things I love. *Lord, don't let it happen to them!* And I have to pull myself together and *do* something. It's just healthier for me to be active. And there's always a chance, according to a Chinese proverb, that an ounce of weight may determine the direction of a ton of matter. *But it must be in the right place at the right time.* To make our actions account for something besides our temporary sanity, we need to determine where, when and what will really count when we win permanent peace.

In my own opinion after more than fifty years in the peace movement, the most critical task today is to abolish war by moving from this global wild-west-with-nuclear-bombs to a governed world where civilized means for settling conflicts among nations can be enforced. I believe what Einstein concluded years ago that "There is no salvation for civilization, and even the human race, other than the creation of a world government with security on the basis of law."

Obstacles still exist to the realization of Einstein's vision. A major factor is the entrenched Military Industrial Complex *worldwide,* which contributes significantly to dysfunctions of the economy and rape of the environment. Other obstacles include the bitter legacy of ethnic strife and the sheer apathy of an affluent minority. Yet, I find reasons to be hopeful on this journey to a governed world.

After all, in my lifetime there has been, **along the High Road,** an end to the empires of Germany, Italy, Britain, France, Japan and the U.S.S.R., and their replacement by voluntary associations of states in Europe, Africa, Southeast Asia, the Americas, and the U.S.S.R. The idea of a constitution as the basis of government has become accepted around the world and federal constitutions have been adopted by many countries. The transformation of Europe from a battleground to a place of prosperity and peace demonstrates to other associations the advantages of a common structure. With a directly elected Parliament and progress toward a federal union, the European Community may even became a model of what the world could be. Opportunities abound in the final decade of this century, designated "Decade of International Law," to speed the momentum toward a governed world:

- The United Nations Conference on Environment and Development in 1992
- the 50th anniversary of the founding of the United Nations in 1995
- the 50th anniversary of the Universal Declaration of Human Rights in 1998
- the 100th anniversary of The Hague Conference outlawing

149

weapons of mass destruciton in 1999
- and the beginning of a new century, a "new way of thinking" (Einstein) and a"New World Order Under Law" (Gorbachev and Bush) in 2000

Along the Low Road there has been, in my observation, a distinguishable rise in consciousness among people, especially the young, in all parts of the world. This appears to be part of some creative evolutionary process, as well as the result of remarkable advances in media technology. It is evident in an explosion of conscience regarding human rights for women, blacks, gays, other minorities, and "liberation" even for animals and plants. Special-interest, non-governmental organizations have multiplied and formed networks of related concerns for peace, justice, jobs, and the environment. One such network in the USA is the Alliance for Our Common Future formed of 50 organizations in 1989 to develop strategies for promoting their common agenda, "to foster human values and respect for nature worldwide...and help to create the moral and political climate in which just and effective structures for peace can develop and endure."

The rate of change is accelerating rapidly. Democracy is on the march. The peace movement is now in the main stream. Millions of business and professional people in the worldwide service club movements such as Rotary, Lions, and Kiwanis are developing a global awareness and a sense of responsible world citizenship. Human rights proponents such as Amesty International and hundreds of ecological groups also promote peace with justice. As these concerns of people become incorporated in institutions of goverment like the European Parliament and a "People's House" in the United Nations, the **Low Road** and the **High Road** converge, and the goal of a democratic federal world government seems almost within reach.

"In The Spirit of San Francisco"

The Stockholm Initiative on Global Security and Governance proposes that a World Summit on Global Governance be called, similar to the meetings in San Francisco and at Bretton Woods in the 1940's. Combining the work of other commissions such as the

Brandt, Palme and Brundtland Commissions, it would present a historical opportunity "not seen since the creation of the United Nations. It must not be lost. Nations must seize it. They must live up to their common responsibility in determining the future of human-kind."[1]

As we prepare for a new century, can we take advantage of these and other opportunites to apply our individual and collective energies effectively in the light of these critical times? My vision is that, in the tradition of those who helped to shape one civilized nation out of feuding colonies, we in our time will take an active role in shaping one civilized world community with liberty and justice, peace, and a healthy environment for all the inhabitants of our world.

1. from *Common Responsibility in the 1990's: The Stockholm Initiative on Global Security and Governance*. Stockholm, Sweden, 1991. Page 42

APPENDIX

A. ORGANIZATIONS ACTIVE IN PROMOTING A DEMOCRATIC FEDERAL WORLD GOVERNMENT

Association of World Citizens
110 Sutter Street, Suite 708
San Francisco, CA 94104, USA
Phone: (415) 989-8717

Association to Unite the Democracies
1506 Pennsylvania Ave., SE, Washington, D.C. 20003, USA
Phone: (202) 544-5150

Campaign for UN Reform
419 7th Street, SE, Washington, D.C. 20003, USA
Phone: (202) 546-3956

Campaign for World Government
552 Lincoln Avenue, Winnetka, IL 60093, USA
Phone: (312) 446-7177 or 835-1377

Canadian Peace Research Institute
25 Dundana Avenue, Dundas, Ontario L9H 4E5, Canada
Phone: (416) 628-2356

Citizens Global Action/The Federalist Caucus
P.O. Box 19742
Portland, OR 97219, USA
Phone: (503) 228-6736

International Network for a UN Second Assembly/CAMDUN (Conferences on a More Democratic United Nations)
301 E. 45th Street, New York, NY 10017, USA
Phone: (212) 983-3353 or
601 Holloway Road, London N19 4DJ, United Kingdom
Phone: 071 272-0024

International Registry of World Citizens/Congres des Peuples
15 Rue Victor Duruy, 75015 Paris, France
Phone: 4531-29-99

World Constitution and Parliament Association
1480 Hoyt Street, Suite 31, Lakewood, CO 80215, USA
Phone: (303) 233-3548

World Federalist Movement
Leliegracht 21, 1016 GR, Amsterdam, The Netherlands
Phone: (020)227502 or UN Office: (212) 599-1320
Branches in the USA: 1-800-HATE WAR; in Canada: (613) 232-0647;
Australia; GPO Box 4878, Sydney, NSW 2001, and other countries

World Government Organization Coalition
8965 Tolhurst Street, Montreal, Quebec H2N 1W9, Canada
Phone (514) 388-7445

SUBJECT INDEX

A

Abolitionist Movement, 19th C
69-79, New A 80-84

Abolition of War 58-59, 62,
69-70

Academy of World Studies
61, 69

Aeschylus 58, 119

Alliance for Our Common
Future 150

Amnesty International 150

Anatomy of Peace, by Emery
Reves 14, 103, 139

Articles of Confederation 29

Association of World Citizens
153

Association to Unite the
Democracies 153

B

Bicentennial, US 87, 103

C

CAMDUN 153

Campaign for UN Reform 153

Campaign for World Government 153

Canadian Peace Research
Institute 153

Citizens Global Action 153

Confederacy to Federal Government 64-65

*Constitution for The Federation
of Earth* 20, 35, 46, 90,
100, 133-135

Constitution, US 106-111, 120
(bibliography), 124-5, 142;
other countries 111-115

Constitutions, World 35, 126-
135, 139 (bibliography)

Convergence, (High Road and
Low Road) 42-47, 150

Court of Man 54

Cousins, Norman 117-118

Covenants 122, 34

D

Decade of International Law
137, 149

Defense Monitor, The 116-117

Democracy Movements iv,
138, 144

Durland, William, *The Illegality
of War* 51-52

E

Ecology 21, 90, 92; Ecological
Imperative 22-24

Economy (of the people, by the
people, for the people) 143

Education (world) 91

Emergency Peace Campaign iii

Emergency World Government
20, 30

European Community 65, 114-115, 136, 149

F

Farris, Joseph cartoon 50
Federalist Caucus 99, 153

G

Global Education Associates 91
Gorbachev, Mikhail 136, 66
and Bush 138, 150

H

High Road 43, 149-150
Hiroshima 95, 147
Human Rights, Universal Declaration of 90

I

Illegality of War by William Durland 51-52
Interdependence, Declarations of 35, 88-89; 91-93
International Network for a UN 2nd Assembly 153
International Registry of World Citizens 153

K

Kant, Immanuel 123-124

L

Law, Decade of International 149; Legal Precedents 56

See World Law
Locke, John 9, 122-123, 141
Low Road 43-44, 150

M

Mauldin Bill, cartoon 6
Mobilization for Survival 45
Mutual Assured Destruction (MAD) iv

N

New Abolitionists 80-84
New World Order ii, 34, 136, 144, 150
NGO's (Non-Government Organizations) 45
Nuremberg Tribunal ii, 53; Principles 56

P

Parliamentarians Global Action 99
Peace Movement 1-2, 147
Peoples Assembly 37-39, 47, 138
Peoples World Parliament 29-30
Plato 121, 141
Prometheus 59

R

Reality Gap 95-97
Rehearsal for World Federation 103, 110-115
Rehearsal, The Great by Carl Van Doren 103-107
Reves, Emery, *The Anatomy of*

156